Don't Let Your Digital Footprint Kick You in the Butt!

A lesson in what *NOT* to do on the Internet to build your personal brand online.

by
Stephanie T. Humphrey

Copyright © 2020 by Stephanie T. Humphrey.

All rights reserved.

No part of this publication may be reproduced, distributed, or transmitted in any form or by any means, including photocopying, recording, or other electronic or mechanical methods, without the prior written permission of the publisher, except in the case of brief quotations, reviews or references.

Printed in the United States of America

Book design by Providence & Design, LLC

ISBN: 978-0-578-74122-2

TESTIMONIALS

> A must read for every youth, young adult and honestly for every adult. As a therapist, I've seen the shame, anxiety, embarrassment and confusion that people experience when they mismanage their social media. One post can literally change your life (for the worse). Don't Let Your Digital Footprint Kick You in the Butt! is a necessary resource to help guide everyone to recognizing and taking care of their personal brand. With the use of practical tools, examples, and insight by tech & lifestyle expert Stephanie Humphrey, the reader walks away chanting the mantra, "I am a Personal Brand!"

Dr. George James
Author, Speaker, Media & Corporate Consultant at George Talks LLC
Chief Innovation Officer & Licensed Marriage & Family Therapist at Council For Relationships

> When we don't reflect before we communicate online, it reflects poorly on us. Luckily Stephanie Humphrey is here to get others--especially teens--to think before they post and align their online self with their authentic self. Don't Let Your Digital Footprint Kick You In the Butt! is as direct and honest as the title suggests, with Stephanie expertly weaving in helpful activities, case studies, and personal anecdotes about building her own personal identity on social media. This book is perfect for teens, parents, and educators looking to have a frank conversation about being their best digital self.

David Ryan Polgar
Founder of All Tech Is Human &
Member of TikTok's Content Advisory Council

Dedication

To any student reading this: I know the internet can seem like a crazy, scary free-for-all, but I hope this book helps you make a little more sense of how you want to show up online.

Also, thank you to my Mom, my family, and my dearest friends - this book could have never happened without all of you.

CONTENTS

Section One • How Does Your Digital Footprint Lead to Your Personal Brand? p.1

> Do you know how far your digital footprint can reach? Did you know that you have a personal brand? Do you know what SEO is and how it can affect you online? Have you ever heard of the Wayback Machine? There are a lot of things to think about every single time you connect to the internet, and we introduce some of those concepts in this section.

Section Two • What Happens When Your Digital Footprint Takes a Wrong Turn? p.46

> There can be some pretty significant consequences to failing to manage your digital footprint in a positive way online. Students are losing opportunities and much worse. We'll take a look at some real-world examples to help you understand what can happen when you're not thinking about how your personal brand is represented online.

Section Three • How to Make Sure Your Digital Footprint Is on the Right Path p.81

> There are specific things you can do to create a good personal brand online and become a responsible digital citizen, and we highlight some of those steps here. Also, it's never too early to think about your LinkedIn presence either, so we give you some tips on how to set up your account and use the platform effectively. You can turn your digital footprint in a positive direction, and we'll show you how!

SECTION ONE

How Does Your Digital Footprint Lead to Your Personal Brand?

footprint [**foot**-print] (noun): a unique set of characteristics, actions, etc., that leave a trace and serve as a means of identification:
ex. Be careful when you post on social media — your online footprint could harm your reputation.

Would you look at that?! Even dictionary.com knows that the internet and social media can potentially be harmful to you. Under most other circumstances, a footprint eventually fades or gets washed away (unless you live on the moon!). But online, everything you do is saved, recorded or can be recovered in some way. The things you do online get stored on multiple servers so deletion is never necessarily permanent, internet archives save websites forever, and technology exists that can save keystrokes — so a record can be kept of the things that you don't post as well as the things you do. At a minimum, a simple screenshot can do more damage than you might think. Your digital footprint is an indelible part of the World Wide Web that makes up a big part of your personal brand. But before you roll your eyes at yet another attempt to get you to stop posting stuff online, keep reading for a little bit. There might be a few different things you haven't thought about as it relates to your online activity, and that's all this book is designed to do — to get you to think before you post. Not to get you to stop posting and not to tell you what to post, but to help you understand that what you do post has an effect on you and others, so it's worth it to take a second to think about it before you put anything out there.

This book was created from a workshop called 'Til Death Do You Tweet. The workshop has that title because that's the one key takeaway from it and from this book. If you don't remember anything else you read here, remember that anything you put online will be there forever — or at least for as long as the internet exists. Does knowing that make a difference in what you decide to share? It should, because everything you put online becomes a part of two things you can't erase — your digital footprint and your personal brand. And those two things are what we'll be focusing on in this section of the book. Let's take the second one first and have a conversation about **branding**.

Your Personal Brand

When you hear the word "brand" what do you think of? Like for instance, if someone says, "I only wear brand-name shoes," what types of shoes would you assume that they wear? You most likely think of a company when you hear the word "brand."

ACTIVITY

Let's do a quick exercise

List three (3) companies below that you're familiar with. Then answer the following questions:

1. _____
2. _____
3. _____

What are the characteristics associated with the company?

_____
_____
_____
_____

What do they make/sell?

_____
_____
_____

What is their logo (if they have one) / What colors are in the logo?

_____
_____
_____

What is the company slogan (if they have one)? Does the company have a theme song?

_____
_____
_____

Who is a spokesperson for the company?

_____
_____

What makes the company memorable to you?

_____
_____
_____

What does the company stand for?

_____
_____
_____

> As you can see in the exercise, there are a lot of things that make up a company's brand. However, companies aren't the only entities that have brands associated with them. People can have their own brands too.

ACTIVITY

Let's try the same branding exercise again.

Name three (3) people who have a brand. They can be celebrities, influencers or whoever is someone who is a part of the public consciousness. Then answer the following questions:

1 • _____
2 • _____
3 • _____

What is the person known/famous for?

_____
_____
_____

Does the person have any special skills or talents?

_____
_____
_____

Does the person have any physical characteristics that define their brand? Does the way they dress define their brand?

_____
_____
_____

What makes the person memorable?

_____
_____
_____
_____

Why do you think people care about the person (whether they love them or hate them)?

_____
_____
_____
_____

Think about what happens when you interact with a company or a person who has a brand you like. You might buy or wear their products, you go to their concerts or download their music, you subscribe to their YouTube channel, you recommend them to people, or you follow them and share their content on social media. You are supporting that company or person in their efforts to build their brand because any time you do any of those things, you are contributing to that company's or that person's brand in a way that helps them grow.

Now think about what can happen when you interact with a company or person who has a brand that you don't like. You won't spend money on anything they offer. If it's a politician, you don't vote for them. You might share content on social media showing why you think their brand is harmful. You might even organize a boycott or protest of the company or person if you feel strongly enough about how their brand is negatively affecting society.

The point is that brands have a strong emotional effect on all of us. They can make us feel happy and inspired or angry and discouraged.

Now think about the fact that we ALL have a brand that has an effect on the people around us. Yes, even you reading this — you have a brand! Whether you choose to acknowledge it or not doesn't really change the fact that your personal brand exists — nor does it matter whether you're a college student, a senior in high school or a sixth-grader. Even if you never do anything to promote your brand, that still doesn't erase it from people's memories. That's because the same way that company brands are represented by the different characteristics you listed in the earlier exercise, your personal brand is also represented in different ways.

How is my brand represented?

The first and most immediate way your brand is represented is in person. There's an old saying that "you never get a second chance to make a first impression," and there's a reason for that. Some research has shown that you have less than one second to make an impression on someone when you meet them in person.

In that short time, you are being judged on your appearance, posture, whether or not you smile, your handshake, how you speak and a lot of other things that you may or may not have any control over. The one thing you do have control over is your attitude. A positive attitude goes a really long way in representing your brand in person. People generally respond to the energy that is presented to them from others. If you present yourself in a friendly, respectful and approachable way, people will usually respond in kind. Not always — some people you meet are determined to be unpleasant (for whatever reason), no matter what you do or say to them. But I can tell you that it's been the case for me more often than not that when I approach a person with positive energy, I typically get that same energy back in return.

It's important to represent your brand well in person because you never know how an opportunity will show up. You can meet someone today who has the potential to change your life, but if your interaction with them is negative — or at least they perceive your interaction with them as negative — it could cause you to lose out on a possible opportunity. This doesn't mean that you should treat everyone you meet nicely because you think they can do something for you. But you should try to approach every initial interaction you have with someone you don't know in a positive way. Even if you never see that person again, they may remember you, and if they have any influence over a future opportunity on your behalf, their first impression of you could make all the difference.

I went to college at Florida A&M University on a full academic scholarship. During my senior year in high school, the president of the university at the time, Dr. Frederick S. Humphries (no relation), was in my hometown to present an information session on the school and called me to invite my family to attend. Because I wasn't representing my brand well at the time, not only did I not take the call because I didn't want to be late to a basketball game, I didn't call him back either! And because I didn't return his phone call, I also did not attend the info session. Now at this point, it would have been perfectly reasonable for Dr. Humphries to make the decision to move on to another student — I probably would have done that myself in his situation. But I was extremely fortunate that he decided to give it another try. He called me one more time at my home before he left town and offered me a full scholarship. To this day I am so thankful that he made that effort and that I finally had the good sense to pick up the phone!

Although we didn't meet face to face at the time, my initial interaction with Dr. Humphries didn't go very smoothly, and it definitely wasn't the best representation of my personal brand that I'd want him to have. I didn't know at the time that he was planning to offer me a scholarship — I just knew that I had other colleges in mind, so I didn't take his phone calls seriously. It was a huge error in judgment that could have cost me a free education. And even if I didn't end up attending Florida A&M anyway, the idea that there was an actual university president out there somewhere who only knew of me because I blew him off makes me shudder to think about to this day. Thankfully, I had worked hard in school and tested well so that the rest of my personal brand was enough to make a decent impression, but that certainly wasn't guaranteed. I learned a very valuable lesson about how the way you show up to something can literally change your life. How are you showing up in person every day?

The second way your brand is represented is in writing. Your written communication can help or harm your personal brand pretty easily. Spelling/grammar errors, typos and informal language or slang might be OK for the text messages you share with your friends, but your homework shouldn't look the same as the group chat! All of our phones have some sort of spell check built in, so there's really no excuse anymore. Your handwriting also plays a part in your written communication, so make sure it's legible. The way you represent your brand in writing lets people know that you care about how you might be perceived, even if you're not standing right in front of someone. I can tell you that when students reach out to me via email or DM, I'm always looking at how well the note is written. It only makes sense to put a little extra effort into your written communication, especially when you're reaching out to ask for something. Also, understand that the tone of your written communication goes a long way as well as your choice of words. It's easy to be misunderstood when you send text messages or email because there isn't always context built in. People may not always receive written messages the way we intend, so it's important to choose your words carefully. We're not going to turn this section into an English lesson, but here's something to think about: Take a look at the last thing you wrote for any class. Would it be something you'd be proud to have represent your personal brand? If not, this might be a good opportunity to ask for some extra help from a teacher or parent if you need it. Good writing skills are going to be essential to have throughout your life so making sure yours are up to par is never a bad idea.

The third way your personal brand is represented is by others. This may not always seem fair, but what other people think of you can have an effect on how you're viewed in general. Think back to that company brand you didn't like. Let's say you were in the Apple Store and you had to wait two hours to get help. You're dissatisfied with the service, so you tweet something negative about your experience and as a result, two of your friends decide not to go to that particular store either. It works the same with personal brands too. If one of your teachers thinks you're the class clown, they might tell other teachers to keep an eye on you because they believe you're prone to bad behavior. You might have only told one joke in class one time, but your brand was solidified in the eyes of that teacher. And now that teacher has influenced others as to who they believe you are — in other words, your personal brand has traveled beyond that specific classroom to others in the school, and it may now be affecting you in a negative way. The same way you influenced your friends not to go to a particular store, even if there was a staff shortage causing delays that day that you didn't know about, is the same way your joke could influence all the teachers you interact with in school, even if it was just that one time. There will be a lot of times when you can't control what other people think of you, but your behavior does make a difference, and it definitely contributes to your personal brand.

Here's another example. Think about someone in your school or neighborhood whom you've never actually met in person, but you're familiar with because of what you've heard about them. Maybe they have a reputation for being unapproachable ("stuck up") or their body language or what they wear makes them seem mean or intimidating. You spend the whole school year avoiding them, listening to rumors and gossip about them. But one day, you have to sit next to them on a field trip. You decide to have a conversation with them and realize that they are actually pretty cool and could even be a friend. You spent a lot of time forming an opinion about them based on what others said and felt and that became a part of their personal brand. It wasn't until you actually talked to them yourself that you realized their brand was totally different than what you thought. That person may just be really shy, but unfortunately because your brand is sometimes represented by what other people think of you, they got a bad reputation. It might take some work to repair your personal brand if it's been damaged by what others think about you. That doesn't mean that you have to go on a campaign to try to get everyone to like you, but you might want to consider feedback from people you trust and make some changes if necessary.

The fourth way your brand is represented is what we'll be focusing on in this book — online. We talk about your personal brand online because it's one of the quickest and most effective ways to establish your brand with a lot of people at the same time. However, it's also one of the quickest and most effective ways to completely destroy your brand in the eyes of a lot of people at the same time as well. We've even given it a term — "cancel culture" — because one post has ruined careers, irreparably damaged brands and unfortunately even cost some people their lives as well.

Cynthia Johnson, author of the book "Platform: The Art and Science of Personal Branding" says you should think of your personal brand like your credit score. It doesn't have control over every aspect of your life, but you need to have a good credit score to do certain things, like buy a house or get a credit card with a good interest rate. Not having any established credit can also hurt your score, and this same concept applies to your personal brand as well. Your behavior as it relates to your personal brand should reflect your efforts to grow and maintain it the same way you improve and maintain your credit score by paying bills on time. A good personal brand will allow your reputation to speak for you in a positive way. This is helpful when you're applying to colleges or for jobs or even trying to get a date. And if someone goes to look for your brand but doesn't find anything — or worse, finds something negative — this can have unfortunate and unintended consequences on your life and the lives of others.

ACTIVITY

Let's do the same exercise as before, but this time we're going to define your brand:

How would you describe your personal brand in one sentence?

_____
_____
_____
_____

What are some physical characteristics people associate with you specifically? Do you dress in a way that people recognize you for?

_____
_____
_____
_____

Are there any personality traits that people recognize you for? (Are you the funny one or the quiet one, etc.)

_____
_____
_____
_____

Are there any talents that people recognize you for? (Do you play sports, or are you the "smart one"? Do you play an instrument or sing/rap?)

_____
_____
_____

What causes do you care about?

_____
_____
_____
_____

How would someone else describe you?

_____
_____
_____
_____

Are the things you're recognized for actually the things you want to be recognized for? If not, what can you do to start to change your personal brand to better reflect who you are?

_____
_____
_____
_____
_____

SECTION ONE

When it comes down to it, your personal brand is what separates you from other people. What makes you unique? If a college recruiter or potential employer had to choose between you and another candidate, what would make you stand out? Your personal brand is what they remember and what they'll use to make their decision. Whether it's how well you answered questions in an interview (your personal brand represented in person) or the follow-up email you sent thanking them for their time (your personal brand represented in writing), the recommendation that your teacher wrote (your personal brand represented by others) or the online search they did, there will be something about your personal brand that will either make or break the opportunity for you. The good news is that you have a lot of control over how your personal brand is represented in all of these areas. With this book, we're going to make sure that your online brand reflects the same positive image that you'd want to represent in person, in writing or by others. I can 100% promise you this: Someone somewhere is going to Google you sooner rather than later (if they haven't already!), and it's your job to make sure that what they find is the best representation of your personal brand that it can be.

Your Digital Footprint

Now let's turn our attention to the concept of a digital footprint. Your digital footprint is any and all of your electronically connected activity — so anything you do that gets transmitted over the internet or a cellular signal. That includes (but is not limited to):

- Social Media
- Email
- Text messages
- Group chat
- YouTube channel
- Website/blog
- Video game streams (Twitch, Discord)
- Google searches
- Online shopping
- Fitness tracker/smartwatch data
- Voice assistant data (like Amazon Echo's Alexa)

Once you've established a digital footprint, that activity contributes to how your personal brand is represented online. Whether you're working on a computer, reading on a tablet or texting on a smartphone, everything you type, share, "Like" or otherwise interact with using Wi-Fi or over a cellular connection is being collected and saved. Because of the high-profile mistakes being committed on a regular basis through social media, the use of social networks tends to overshadow all the other things that make up your digital footprint. But while it is a major factor and probably one of the easiest ways to damage your online reputation, social media is just the tip of the iceberg as it relates to your overall digital use. Every time you post on social media, upload a photo or watch a video, ask Alexa for information or Google your medical symptoms, you are adding to your digital footprint. It's a record of all those emails you sent, those comments you left on that post and the music you downloaded from iTunes. And remember that it also includes that text message you just responded to, the group chat you're included in and the last e-book you read.

Your digital footprint is also made up of stuff you don't necessarily post online yourself too. Did your school paper do a story on you and post it to the school's website? Are your basketball stats searchable on a sports blog? Did someone tag you in a picture on social media? All of those things contribute to your digital footprint as well. Is someone out there right now searching for you specifically and all your digital interactions? Maybe, maybe not. But could someone search for you using any one of these electronic activities? Absolutely. The importance of understanding what you're sharing online — and what's shared about you — cannot be overstated. None of this is to say that you should unplug, go hide in a cave and cut yourself off from the rest of society. It is simply a reminder that your digital footprint leaves tracks across the web that can't be erased, so it's always in your best interest to consider your online actions and what you choose to share. The good news is that there are some things you have some relative control over, so you can avoid a lot of potential negative consequences by following the number one rule on the internet: Think before you post! It's not always the easiest rule to follow, but it is critical to ensuring that you don't end up making a mistake that haunts you for years to come.

Two main characteristics of your digital footprint are that it is searchable AND recoverable. There is always a way to find information once it has been posted online, and if someone can find it, that information can be recovered and shared. I cannot stress enough how important it is for you to understand this concept. You can lead your digital footprint wherever you want it to go across the internet, but it's critical that you do your best to point it in the right direction.

ACTIVITY

Think about all the things you do that are connected to the internet or a cellular connection.

Try to list as many as you can — you might be surprised at how long the list is!

Another aspect of the internet that is directly connected to your digital footprint is the concept of **Search Engine Optimization (SEO)**. Imagine being tasked with the job of taking a simple search query for "sneakers" and having to crawl through literally billions of web pages, documents, images, .pdfs and anything else that lives on the World Wide Web to return a result that is correct and relevant in a fraction of a second. Internet browsers with search engines (Google Chrome, Microsoft Edge, Firefox, Safari, etc.) do this with a speed and accuracy that is simply astonishing. Not only are search engines invested in returning results that are correct and relevant, they are also looking for the most popular websites from which to provide the results. When you search for "Jordans," the first website that comes back is likely to be nike.com. Then you might see footlocker.com, finishline.com, etc. SEO is the magic that makes those search results happen in that order. But determining correctness, relevance and popularity ain't easy! There are hundreds, if not thousands, of variables that search engines take into consideration to figure out what you really want to see when you type a question into that search box. All of the math that goes into the algorithms that make those decisions create "ranking factors" that determine what you see when you press "Enter." And the ever-changing strategies that websites employ to attempt to be the first thing you see make up Search Engine Optimization.

SECTION ONE

Why is it so important to be first? The answer is simple. According to multiple statistics, more than **90% of people** searching online don't look past the first page of the search results. If you think about what happens when you Google something, how often do you click through to the second or third page to see what else pops up? Probably not that often. And, of those 90-percent-plus who never make it to Page 2, **almost half** don't even bother to look past the first three to five links that get returned in the search. This means that websites' fight to get to the top of the search results page is critical to their survival because a webpage that no one visits may as well not exist on the internet at all.

ACTIVITY

First, Google an item — it can be anything, like a product, an idea or a song.

Check out the first three search results for that item (the ones that aren't paid advertisements). Do you think they represent the brand for that item in a positive way?

_____
_____
_____
_____
_____

Next, Google a celebrity, and evaluate the first three search results in the same way.

_____
_____
_____
_____
_____
_____
_____
_____
_____

What does the internet know about you?

When was the last time you Googled yourself? It should be something you do regularly to check up on how your personal brand shows up online. Take a minute and do that now.

What do the first five search results show?

1. _____
2. _____
3. _____
4. _____
5. _____

Is there someone out there with your same name that shows up first?

_____
_____
_____
_____

If so, how is their personal brand reflected online?

_____
_____
_____
_____
_____
_____

What might happen if someone got the two of you confused?

_____
_____
_____
_____
_____
_____
_____
_____
_____
_____

> **Next, research Google Alerts and set one up for yourself so that you'll be notified when new information about you makes its way to the web.**

Search engine optimization can be a big advantage for you as it relates to your own digital footprint. SEO can be complicated and confusing, so there are a lot of websites that don't do it particularly well. And SEO is its own very involved animal, so there are a lot of smaller companies and websites that don't have teams dedicated to optimizing their site, and that don't have the budget to hire digital marketing experts to help. But do you know which websites do have the teams and budget in place to expertly execute SEO? Social networks, web-hosting companies and media outlets. If you have a presence on any social network, that search result probably came up on the first page. If you have your own website, blog or YouTube channel, that search result probably came up on the first page as well. And if you've ever been featured in a print media article or on television, it's likely that search result is on the first page too. What this means is that some of the user-generated information you volunteer on the internet has a lot of influence on what people see when they search for you — which in turn means that you do have some control over your digital footprint online because you contribute the content. Here's a personal example from my own experience of why controlling your narrative online is important:

> I visited a friend of mine a while ago, and in a panic, he asked me for my help with a problem. He works in the entertainment industry, so his personal brand can mean the difference between booking the job and eating ramen noodles that month. We sat down, and he pulled out his laptop — but I was totally unprepared for what I saw next. Someone had downloaded photos of him from Facebook (or possibly from a Google image search) and posted them to a website — **www.stddirectory.com** —

with a warning to all ladies who might encounter him to stay away because he was a health risk (yes, that "STD"). To add insult to injury, the egregious entry was only discovered after his mom Googled him — and that particular website was the second search result that was returned.

Upon closer examination, it was clear that the website operated in a similar manner as "revenge porn" sites — posts can be made anonymously. Also, "reputation management" services are offered to the victimized parties — to the tune of a hefty fee paid to the owner of the site to remove the offensive content. My friend had already contacted the company and was told that the post could be pulled down for a fee of $1,500. They were only willing to guarantee that the post would remain off the site for one year, implying the expectation of a $1,500 annual fee to keep the content off the internet. The company also suggested that we contact the person who originally made the post, but since it was anonymous, well…you get the point. We did a WHOIS lookup, which allows you to search for information about a specific domain name. Based on the name of the site, we were able to find out some basic info about the owner of the website, but unfortunately there was very little of it. The website was registered to a company outside of the United States, with only a P.O. Box and 1-800-number associated with it.

He is pursuing legal options — an attorney friend is sending a cease and desist letter to the mailing address, and he has reached out to legal organizations that take on revenge porn cases. I also suggested that he file a complaint with HIPPA, considering this website was allowing sensitive medical information (albeit false) to be posted to the site. We were just looking at all our options and trying whatever we thought would work. But then I looked at his own digital activity — there wasn't much to be found considering his occupation. He wasn't very active on social media, didn't have a website, etc. His digital footprint wasn't very big, so my recommendation to him was create one! Based on what I knew about people's browsing habits, I knew that if we couldn't get rid of the search result entirely, at least we could flood the internet with enough of his own content that it might not make a difference. If more than 90% of the public doesn't bother to look past the first page of a search result, even getting the offensive content to Page 3 would be almost like deleting it altogether.

The SEO of social networks is excellent — but only if you actually use them and use them in the way they were intended. That means all your profiles should be com-

plete (with profile pictures, bios, etc.), and you should be engaging with them consistently and posting regular content. The best SEO works because information on websites links to info on other websites, and social networks are one of the best ways to build those links for individuals looking to create a digital footprint. I made sure my friend completed all the profiles of the social networks he was active on and add a few more. And I helped him set up tools that would make posting content a little easier to help him be more consistent online. And he's done some of his own personal brand-building as well, securing press for various projects. After a few weeks, the offending search result was the ninth entry on the first page. And, while nothing ever truly gets deleted from the internet, I'm thrilled to say that the last time I checked — the offensive post was waaaaayyy down on Page 8! The possibility of someone seeing the entry has been dramatically reduced. That's the power of SEO…

If you've ever posted something that you think might not be the best representation of your personal brand, you might be wondering right now, "Well, can't I just delete it and make it go away?" Unfortunately, the answer isn't as simple as that. The internet never forgets, and there is a website designed specifically to make sure that it doesn't. The Wayback Machine is a digital archive of the World Wide Web that was launched in 2001, but it had been caching (storing) web pages as far back as 1996. For many internet users, that timeframe fully encapsulates their entire online presence. The archive uses software to crawl the web and store publicly available web pages that aren't blocked or password-protected. This means that if your social media profiles are set to "Private," they won't be saved. But if they were public at any time or are public now, there is most likely an archive of them on this site. To date, there are approximately a half trillion web pages stored on the site, and that number is growing every day. And while not every web page on the internet gets archived, and pages may only be archived from specific time periods, having access to that type of information can still get you in a lot of trouble.

Here's an example of just how an old post can come back to haunt you:

> MSNBC host Joy Reid faced some very serious allegations and an even more intense social media backlash when seemingly homophobic blog posts she wrote in the mid-to-late 2000s resurfaced recently. The posts were from her blog "The Reid Report," which is now defunct. At first Reid denied the claims, until archived pages of the blog were recovered using the Wayback Machine's digital archive. Once evidence of the blog post was uncovered, Reid then suggested that the digital archive had

been hacked in some way. However, the administrators of the Wayback Machine conducted their own investigation and found no such evidence of any tampering. The social media backlash was swift, and Reid finally did apologize for the content, but it seems that the damage may have already been done. In the three months since the scandal broke, Reid's MSNBC show had double-digit losses in total viewership.

The most important thing to note here is that the pages recovered using the Wayback Machine digital archive were acquired after Reid had already deleted her blog from the internet. Also, while the drop in ratings may not be completely attributable to the controversy, no one can argue that it certainly didn't help. MSNBC has been suspiciously silent about commenting on the situation, and one can't help but wonder if this will affect her tenure with the network going forward. Reid could have potentially avoided a lot of this drama by following the number one rule of the internet — think before you post!

ACTIVITY

Go to the Wayback Machine — www.archive.org/web

Enter the URL (web address) of one of your public social media profiles. How many times has the Wayback Machine archived that page?

_____
_____

Take a look at some of the earlier dates that were saved and check out your profile from that time. Is there anything there that might not be the most positive representation of your personal brand?

_____
_____
_____
_____
_____
_____
_____
_____
_____
_____
_____

When we talk about a digital footprint as it relates to a personal brand, we tend to focus on social media almost exclusively because it's one of the quickest ways to grow and maintain a personal brand online while simultaneously being one of the quickest ways to destroy a personal brand online at the same time. But remember, your digital footprint extends beyond your social media activity. It includes ALL of your internet-connected activity. Think about the celebrity iCloud hack of 2014. Dozens of celebrities, including Jennifer Lawrence, Gabrielle Union, and Kirsten Dunst among others had nude photos leaked to the internet. The hack was high-profile enough to warrant an FBI investigation, and as of August 2018 four people had been arrested, convicted and sent to prison as a result.

The obvious point here is that none of those photos was

posted to any social media platform. The pictures in question were taken using victims' smartphones and information obtained through phishing scams enabled the hackers to gain access to them. But I wonder how many of those celebrities even knew that their photos were being automatically uploaded to their iCloud accounts in the first place? Did they know that feature was turned on by default but could have been disabled? If the photos in question had only been stored locally on the phone that was used to take the picture, as I'm inclined to believe at least some of the victims thought was the case, the pictures could have only been obtained by someone with physical access to the device. Because the photos were uploaded to iCloud accounts, they became a part of those users' internet-connected activities and thus their digital footprints as well. Using iCloud as a service isn't inherently bad — it's an effective way to store photos in the event that your smartphone gets lost, stolen or damaged, and it allows you to access those photos from different devices by connecting to the internet. However, knowing that the automatic upload feature was turned on by default might have prompted different decision-making about the type of pictures that were taken in the first place or at least some extra care could have been taken to secure them. This example is not about what type of photos you should and should not take — although if you are a minor, taking nude photos of yourself or possessing nude photos of another minor is illegal, and we'll talk about why in Section Two. My only goal right now is to highlight the fact that it's critical to consider your entire digital footprint in building your personal brand online. FYI — if you want to turn off the automatic uploads to iCloud, the following screenshots show you how:

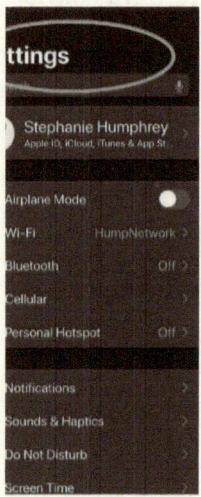  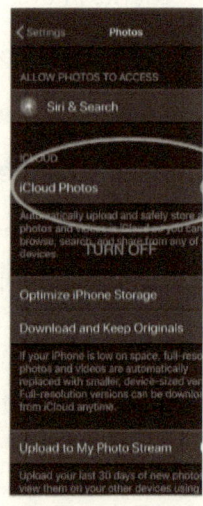

And finally, do you know what information the companies that run different social networks know and save about you? How many of you have actually read the terms of service (TOS) of any website you've used? Don't feel too bad if you haven't, most of us don't bother either. According to a 2017 study by Deloitte, 91% of people accept TOS without reading the agreement. This number jumps to 98% for users aged 18-34 years old. And would it really matter anyway, considering you can't use the service if you don't agree to the terms? None of the social networks or other services we use online allow us to accept their TOS conditionally — it's an all or nothing proposition. And with the way our lives are connected digitally these days, most of us can't afford not to have an email account or a Facebook page. However, an understanding of how your data is being used online should have some impact on what you choose to share and which sites you choose to share with. Recently, websites have been making an attempt to present their TOS in language that is easy to understand so even a cursory read-through will provide you with at least some insight on their use of your data.

So, let's check it out. We'll use Snapchat as an example, because that social network made a name for itself because they let you send messages that "disappeared" after a certain amount of time. But even with a service that claims self-destructing messages, there's always the fine print.

The first thing you want to understand is that the company reserves the right to use anything you upload or post in any way they see fit. Per Snapchat's TOS:

> "Many of our Services let you create, upload, post, send, receive, and store content. When you do that, you retain whatever ownership rights in that content you had to begin with. But you grant us a license to use that content... For all content you submit to the Services other than Public Content, you grant Snap Inc. and our affiliates a worldwide, royalty-free, sublicensable, and transferable

> *license to host, store, use, display, reproduce, modify, adapt, edit, publish, and distribute that content..."*

What stands out here is the fact that you're granting the rights to your data to Snapchat and their *affiliates* with a license that is *sub-licensable* and *transferable*. If this doesn't automatically raise your eyebrows, think Cambridge Analytica. The company at the center of the Facebook 2016 election scandal was an affiliate of Facebook who was permitted access to your data and your friends' data via Facebook's TOS. And again, while you don't have much choice about how Facebook chose to share your data if you want to use the service, you may have thought twice about taking the personality quiz that Cambridge Analytica used if you had known what else you'd have to give up. Let's look at an interesting passage of Snapchat's privacy policy concerning data deletion:

> *"Keep in mind that, while our systems are designed to carry out our deletion practices automatically, we cannot promise that deletion will occur within a specific timeframe. There may be legal requirements to store your data and we may need to suspend those deletion practices if we receive valid legal process asking us to preserve content or if we receive reports of abuse or other Terms of Service violations. Finally, we may also retain certain information in backup for a limited period of time or as required by law."*

So, Snapchat will try to delete your information in a timely fashion if requested, but they cannot guarantee that it "will occur within a specific timeline." They've also just let you know that they can save your data indefinitely for the purposes of making it available to law enforcement or some other legal procedure if necessary. And if anyone decides to take offense to something you've posted and reports you for abuse, that data can also be saved indefinitely, regardless of the context in which you posted it. The way this reads, you don't really have any guarantee that your data will ever be deleted from Snapchat's servers. Your digital footprint really does have the potential to live online forever. And circling back to those five-second, self-destructing Snaps — Snapchat even saves those for 30 days if none of the persons you sent them to opens them within that timeframe. A lot can happen online in a month…

The goal here is not to paint social networks or other online services as some kind of boogeyman and scare you off them entirely. The idea is simply to get you to pause before you post and really think about whether that information needs to be shared because once you put it out there, you most likely can never take it back. It all becomes a part of your digital footprint and leaves indelible tracks across the web. I'll be repeating the number one rule of the internet throughout this book — **think before you post!**

ACTIVITY

Research Instagram's privacy policy.

What are they allowed to do with your data and who are they allowed to share your photos/content with?

_____
_____
_____
_____
_____
_____
_____
_____
_____
_____

How can you delete your account?

_____
_____
_____
_____
_____
_____
_____
_____

SECTION ONE | ACTIVITY

How can you request a download of your information?

_____
_____
_____
_____
_____
_____
_____

Is there anything else in their privacy policy that stands out to you?

_____
_____
_____
_____
_____
_____
_____
_____
_____

And for all those of you out there that are reading this and thinking, "I don't have any social media, so my digital footprint should be safe, right?" That's not exactly true either. If you've never owned a computer, tablet or smartphone or have never interacted with the internet in any way on any device I might say you had a chance. But even then, public records exist and have been digitized, and these days the likelihood that someone you know is active online and has posted a picture of you on social media or otherwise identified you as a friend or relative is very high. I don't know that I've ever seen my father touch a computer keyboard in my life, but in a rudimentary search of his name I was able to find his date of birth, home address and my name listed as his daughter along with my siblings. But he does have a smartphone, so the metadata attached to his text messages and photos is up for grabs, and he also has a smartwatch that monitors his golf game, so now information about his swing is a part of his digital footprint too. In much the same way you used to be able to find out someone's phone number and address from a phone book, you can uncover lots of personal details about them online. There are also dozens of internet "people search" engines with new ones popping up every day. One way or another, your digital footprint likely exists.

But you also want to think about what not having much of an online presence says about your personal brand too. An employer or college recruiter might think you weren't as tech savvy as your peers. You're also leaving your brand up to the random results of a Google search. What if someone with the same or a similar name as you has an arrest record? Or that person is a porn star or is known for saying racist things online? They would likely appear in search results instead of you and the possibility that someone — like a college recruiter or potential employer

— could confuse you for them is high. We all know that people don't usually click on links to actually read articles. They see a headline and assume they know the rest. And most people won't search for too long either. We already talked about the fact that studies have shown around 98% of people don't look past the first page of Google search results. That means if there was something about you buried down on Page 4, it would basically be invisible to most people. Remember the example about my friend and SEO? You want to use the internet and social media to your advantage to develop, grow and maintain your personal brand, and that starts with being active on it.

If you're not on social media because your parents have said you were too young to have an account, **you should listen to them**. You might not be able to have an account yet, but it's not too soon to talk to them about your digital footprint and how you should manage it online. You could even show them this book and have them help you with the next activity:

ACTIVITY

If you don't have any online presence that you've put there yourself (website/blog, YouTube channel, social media, etc.), think about one thing you might want to create on the internet to start building your digital footprint and personal brand.

Will it be a social media page, personal website, YouTube channel or something else?

_____
_____
_____

What will you use it for mostly? To keep in touch with family/friends, showcase your work or something else?

_____
_____
_____
_____

Who will you be connected to? Who can friend/follow you and who can you friend/follow?

_____
_____
_____
_____

SECTION ONE | ACTIVITY

Will your parent/guardian be your friend or follow you on the account? Will they be able to see what you post?

_____
_____
_____
_____
_____

What will you do if a stranger tries to contact you or sends you a message?

_____
_____
_____
_____
_____

How often will you get to use the account?

_____
_____
_____
_____
_____

What are some things you could post that would cause you to lose your privileges to the account and damage your personal brand?

_____
_____
_____
_____
_____

SECTION TWO

When Your Digital Footprint Takes a Wrong Turn

If you're still wondering why building a positive personal brand matters, we're going to use this section to take a look at a few case studies that will illustrate what can happen when you don't think about how your digital footprint affects your brand. Whether it's a lost opportunity for school, for a job or worse, there are very real, negative consequences to not representing your brand in a positive way online.

Why do you think people post negative things online? I believe the idea of perceived *anonymity* plays a role in understanding some digital behavior. Psychologist John Suler coined the term *"online disinhibition effect,"* which is the theory that once you're able to become detached from your identity, you could also detach yourself from some normal societal constraints on your behavior. This can go in a couple of ways: you may become much more vulnerable online, sharing things with strangers you would never tell your best friend in real life. Services like Tumblr have been literal lifesavers for people to connect with others who have shared experiences in real life. Or, emboldened by a perceived lack of consequence, you could become the most hated thing on the internet — a troll. An internet troll is someone who uses deliberately offensive and inflammatory language online for the express purpose of provoking an argument with other users. Trolling can also extend into harassment and other negative behaviors as well but is routinely regarded as behavior that would never manifest itself (or be tolerated) in real life.

You have to understand that even though you might think you're getting away with something because you believe no one knows who you are on the internet, there are consequences to everything you do — in real life and online. And even with the strongest privacy settings or fake accounts, your digital behavior can still be discovered and traced back to you. The best way to approach anything you do online is to remember your personal brand and think before you post!

Justine Sacco

One thing you want to understand — well, after you understand that everything that you post online will be there forever — is that you don't have to have a lot of followers for your posts to get you in trouble. Things go viral on the internet all the time, for good and bad reasons. In 2013 Justine Sacco, a woman with only 170 Twitter followers at the time, became the top trending Twitter topic in the world. She posted a few racially insensitive tweets before she boarded a plane that she would go on to describe as "jokes." Eleven hours later, the hashtag #HasJustineLandedYet was the most talked about story on the web. Even though she had no idea what was happening, Justine was fired by the time her plane landed and endured endless taunts and even death threats. Lots of articles were written about her as well that will now be a permanent part of her digital footprint. Any time anyone Googles her name, she will forever be connected to this story. Take a minute to Google her right now and read some of the articles about how this one incident completely changed her life. Justine wasn't famous or a well-known celebrity, but her content was still able to spread across the web like wildfire. Even with just a few followers, the chance that your content could be seen by thousands or even millions of people is always a possibility.

Emily Clow / Kickass Masterminds

But sometimes your content only needs to be seen by one person to cause unintended consequences. In 2019, 24-year-old Emily Clow applied for a position with marketing company Kickass Masterminds. After she applied, she was asked for additional application materials including her social media handles. When the company checked out her Instagram, CEO Sara Christensen posted a picture of Emily in a bikini to the company's Instagram Stories with a snarky caption about what not to post when you're applying for a job. And because of one post, Emily is still searching for that job…

However, in an interesting twist of fate, the CEO and the company also faced backlash online for posting Emily's picture without her permission. They were accused of body shaming and as a result of the negative publicity, had to shut down their website and make their social media accounts private. The CEO also issued a public apology to Emily. However, she still did not hire her…

This example perfectly reinforces the idea from Section One of this book that **we all have a brand**. Whether it's a company's brand or our own personal brand, there is information out there about those brands that people will use to make a determination about who they think you are. It remains to be seen if Kickass Masterminds will lose any clients or have trouble getting new ones, and Emily still doesn't have a job six months after the incident. But it is **very important** that we all consider the potential consequences of how we represent our brands online. Should Emily be ashamed for taking a picture in a bikini? Absolutely not. However, the way in which Emily chose to represent her brand came into conflict with how the company chooses to represent their brand — and in this case, the company won. In reality, there were no winners on either side of this situation, and I hope everyone in this case is more mindful about what they post and how it affects their brands going forward.

ACTIVITY

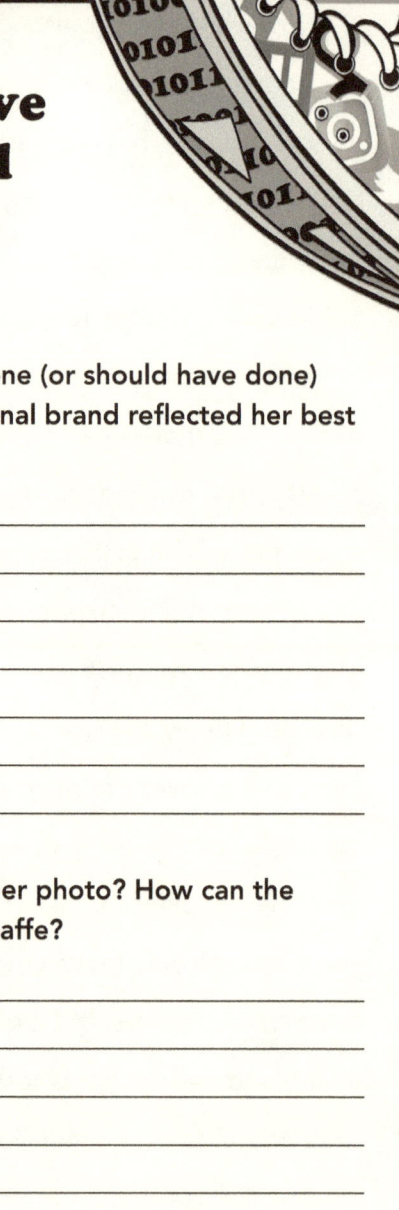

Should Emily have offered her social media handles to the company?

Is there anything she could have done (or should have done) beforehand to make sure her personal brand reflected her best self?

_____
_____
_____
_____
_____
_____
_____

Was the company right in posting her photo? How can the company fix their brand after this gaffe?

_____
_____
_____
_____
_____
_____
_____

Dante Harris

Dante Harris has a personal story that could easily be turned into a TV movie of the week. Starting his life from very humble beginnings in Columbus, Ga., he was virtually homeless as a teen. But he maintained good grades in school and was the captain of the basketball team. A woman named Amber Massey noticed this quiet young man — who was academically excellent but emotionally reserved — and decided to get to know him better. She eventually learned his story and was moved to help him succeed. All of their efforts together were realized when Dante earned a full $70,000 scholarship to the military school at the University of North Georgia in 2015. He was just as good a student in college as he had been in high school — until one bad lapse in judgement threatened to change his life forever.

In November 2016, Dante decided to "play a joke" on one of the school's officials. Dante took a picture of him in a restroom from behind while the official's pants were down and his buttocks were exposed. Dante only shared the picture with three friends, but those friends shared the photo to a group thread with hundreds of other students on it.

The official in the photo turned out to be second in command at the school and decided to press charges against Dante. One of those charges was unlawful surveillance, which is a felony and carries a sentence of up to six years in prison. Dante was also facing the prospect of a six-semester suspension, which could cost him his scholarship. Fortunately, Dante was able to appeal the suspension. He was only suspended for two semesters and his scholarship was not be affected. However, the criminal charges *have not* been dropped, and he still faces a felony in the state of Georgia that could send him to prison for years. He also has his digital footprint and personal brand to think about too — if he wants to continue military service after college, this may definitely hurt his chances. And really any future employer might Google him and see all the articles that were written about the situation and decide he's not a good fit for their company. From this point on, Dante will never know what opportunities he's missed out on because of this one unfortunate decision.

What's the lesson here? First, you need to understand that your idea of humor won't be shared by everyone. So before you tell a joke or pull a prank, it's worth it to think about how someone else might respond first. Second, the moment that your activity becomes digital, it's out of your hands. I am 100% positive that Dante did not mean for that photo to be shared beyond the three friends he initially sent it to. Maybe they all have the same sense of humor, and he thought they would get a laugh and that would be the end of it. But once you send something electronically, you've sent it into cyberspace and it now has the potential to end up virtually anywhere. Dante also failed to understand the idea of a brand. A military school has a very strict code of conduct and the expectations for students there are higher than they might be at another school. A joke like this may have gotten him a minor reprimand somewhere else (if he had gotten in trouble at all), but the standards of this particular school — standards that are a part of the school's brand — are different. Because his sense of humor — which is a part of his personal brand — conflicted with the school's brand of a certain high standard of behavior, he may now be facing consequences that could forever change his life. Your brand and your digital footprint are inextricably connected — anything you do or say is a part of your personal brand that could become a part of your digital footprint and vice versa.

ACTIVITY

Answer/Discuss the following questions:

Is taking a picture like this ever OK?

_____
_____
_____
_____
_____
_____
_____
_____

How might Dante be able to recover his personal brand after this incident?

_____
_____
_____
_____
_____
_____
_____
_____
_____

It's also important to remember that your brand is represented in more ways than just online. The internet has made memes out of the likes of "BBQ Becky," "Permit Patty," "Pool Patrol Paula" and others, but their behavior and the consequences of that behavior are no laughing matter. Those women (and many other men and women like them) have recently come under fire for calling the police on people of color for reasons that weren't immediately obvious. Some of them reported black people or other people of color for absolutely no reason at all. In some of the cases, racial slurs or other bad language was used. What these people didn't count on was that their actions would be recorded and posted for all the world to see. They probably also didn't anticipate the consequences either — in almost all these cases, the people calling the police were fired from their jobs. They also now have to deal with the fact that these memes and the news stories are forever connected to their digital footprints and their personal brands.

Just about everyone has a smartphone these days, and no one has a problem whipping it out to record you at the most inopportune moment. It's almost as if people are trying to "catch" you doing something regretful so they can be the first one to call you out and post a video. But when you're representing your brand in person in a positive way, you don't give them the chance to put you on blast online. You can't be "canceled" if you don't give anyone a reason.

ACTIVITY

Google the term "BBQ Becky."

How many pages of articles are returned in the search?
___

What do you think of Jennifer Schulte's personal brand now?
___
___
___
___

How might this one incident affect her in the future?
___
___
___
___

What could she have done differently to protect her brand?
___
___
___
___

Another aspect of social media and your online activity you want to understand is that in this day and age, there really is no such thing as privacy anymore. You can do your best to make sure that your privacy settings are locked down on your social media accounts, and you might think you can trust everyone included in the group chat, but the reality is that something you thought was private could potentially be exposed to the world at any point.

Harley Barber

Take the case of 19-year old New Jersey native Harley Barber. In 2018, Harley was a freshman at the University of Alabama and a member of Alpha Phi sorority. She decided to post a couple of extremely offensive videos to her "finsta" (fake Instagram account) using racial slurs and appearing to be unapologetic about her actions. Not only did Harley get expelled from the university, she also got kicked out of the sorority and received death threats as well. This incident is forever connected to her digital footprint and will be a part of her personal brand any time someone searches for her online. A "finsta" is an account that is usually considered very private — a person typically only has a few followers and is only following a few accounts. It's supposed to be the place where people can be their authentic selves online without feeling the pressure to have every picture or video look perfect. Privacy settings for a finsta are generally pretty tight by design — if this is the account that you're using as a platform to share your true self with a few trusted friends, you'd want to make sure that only the people you designate are given access to the feed. But even with that understanding, Harley's posts still managed to go viral. Did Harley just need better friends, or should she have thought about how her personal brand might be affected by posting this type of content? I'd say the answer is probably a bit of both. While you don't have to continue to support friends you think are racist (or continue to be friends with them at all), is it your personal responsibility to expose them to the public? Maybe. If that friend was in a position to make decisions that affect a particular group of people but held stereotypically negative opinions of that group that weren't true, it might be necessary to bring that information to someone's attention. At the same time, Harley should have understood that a reasonable expectation of privacy simply doesn't exist anymore, and she should have considered the potential negative impact to her brand that could be caused if someone outside of her followers got access to the content. Unfortunately, it's not always an "either or" proposition.

One other unintended consequence of this whole situation was that Harley wasn't the only one negatively affected by her posts. When the story made national news, her mom was also on the receiving end of negative and threatening online comments. People assumed that "the apple doesn't fall far from the tree" — meaning that if Harley had those opinions, then she was probably raised by a parent who thought the same way (which her mom says is absolutely not true). Harley's mom also believes that this incident will have a negative effect on her 10-year-old sister as well. How crazy is it that a couple of posts to a private account have wreaked havoc on an entire family? Sometimes, your personal brand isn't just about you. It's critical to think about how what you do online affects others in real life.

But TechLifeSteph, what about free speech??? I get this question ALLLLL the time, and my answer is always the same. We live in the United States of America, and there is some language in the Constitution about all citizens having the right to "freedom of speech." But do you know what that really means? The First Amendment to the Constitution states:

> *"Congress shall make no law respecting an establishment of religion, or prohibiting the free exercise thereof; or abridging the freedom of speech, or of the press; or the right of the people peaceably to assemble, and to petition the Government for a redress of grievances."*

That's what the First Amendment says — but what does that actually mean? Simply put, it means that our government cannot make a law that says you have to worship a certain way or that you can't worship the way you choose. It also says that our government cannot abridge — which in this case means curtail by law — our right to speak freely. That right to speak freely also applies to our news and media as well. And finally it says that our government cannot restrict your right to peacefully assemble in protest (or for any other reason), and you can petition the government if you have an issue with something they've done. What's the one common theme running throughout the amendment? If you guessed "the government," you're right. These are things that our government cannot do to its citizens, i.e., you. And even more specifically, these are things that you can't be put in jail for by our government. However, these restrictions only apply to our government. If a college doesn't want you to use racist language as a condition of attending that school, they are well within their rights to deny you admission. They are also allowed to expel you from school for the things you say or write as well. The same goes for an employer too. If you do, say or write something that goes against company policy, they have every right to take whatever action they feel is appropriate to protect their company brand. You haven't been denied the ability to speak your mind. Your Twitter fingers can spring into action any time you feel like it and say pretty much anything you want online (with the exception of threats and things like that). But just because you can say what you want doesn't mean there aren't consequences to what you say. You're not necessarily going to end up in prison for what you say, but sometimes free speech still might cost you...

SECTION TWO

One thing I hope you understand from these case studies is that at some point, your personal brand is going to be connected to someone else's in some way. Unless you plan to live off the grid in the mountains by yourself, you're eventually going to want to go to college or some other school, you're going to have to get a job (or if you start your own business you'll need paying clients), you'll want to be in a relationship, buy a house/car, and the list goes on and on. To be a part of the society we live in, your personal brand will be connected to the brands of other people and companies constantly. Any time you walk into a place of business, the way you represent your brand in person gets connected to the business's brand — and if you behave in a way that conflicts with that brand you can be kicked out. For example, you might be able to get away with being loud and rowdy at a concert, and that behavior might even be encouraged. But at a library, the same behavior will most likely result in you being asked to leave. The same thing happens online too. You might get into an argument with someone on Twitter and use a lot of "colorful" language without much consequence. But if you were to send an email to Amazon's customer service representing your brand in the same way, you might not get the result you expect. When there is a conflict between your brand and someone else's, the person or entity with the strongest brand usually wins out, but not all the time. Even if you win a "battle of the brands" against someone else, there's still the possibility that someone close to you will be affected by your brand too. Maintaining a positive personal brand in real life and online won't necessarily guarantee you'll never come into conflict with anyone else, but it's certainly a good place to start. Protect your brand!

Cyber Bullying

Let's turn our attention to cyber bullying. Even if it is not happening to you right now, and hasn't happened to anyone you know, cyber bullying is a real thing and is negatively affecting a lot of students (and adults) across the country and around the world. But what is cyber bullying?

> *Cyber bullying is bullying that takes place over digital devices. It involves sending, posting or sharing content that is negative, threatening, harmful, false or contains someone's personal information.*

It can be hard sometimes to know if you're bullying someone because you might not think that what you're doing is that bad. Or you might think that that other person should be able to "take a joke." But what is important for you to understand is that everyone has different mental and emotional capabilities the same way people have different physical capabilities. You might be able to run faster than one person, but you can't do as may push-ups as someone else. In the same way, someone else might not be able to psychologically process bullying the same way you might. You might just "shake it off" and go about the rest of your day like normal. But someone else may not be able to forget about it so easily, and they might take it seriously enough to want to harm themselves or others because of it. The point is that you can't ever really know how someone is going to respond to something you do or say about them online.

Channing Smith

On September 23, 2019, 16-year-old Channing Smith took his own life after he was outed as bisexual online. He had previously sent text messages to one boy who forwarded screenshots to someone else. That person then posted the messages online and all of the negative comments and responses proved to be too much for Channing to handle. We can look back and talk about what Channing should and should not have shared, but that would be missing the point. He shared something personal with someone he thought he could trust. Was he just never supposed to trust anyone again ever? The point is that this situation should have never happened in the first place.

Think about your deepest darkest secret. Or even just something about yourself that you might be insecure about. That thing that makes you feel awkward around other people because you feel like they might be judging you about it. That thing that might have kept you from joining a team or auditioning for a school play or running for student government because you were worried about what people might say about you. We all have that. Thing. That thing that keeps us up at night. That one thing that, if it were different, you feel like your whole life would be better. Even if it seems trivial, like maybe you wish you could afford to wear the same type of clothes as some other people in your school. If it bothers you and makes you uncomfortable, it's a valid thing. You're doing your best to deal with it, but it's not something you want the whole world to know about.

Now think about what would happen if you told your best friend. They might support you (or at least they should) and offer you words of encouragement. It might not be that bad for them to know because now you feel like you don't have to carry that thing around by yourself all the time — because it can get really heavy sometimes. But what would happen if that thing got out to five other people in your school? That might even be OK — or at least you could deal with it — because five isn't really that many people, and the five people who know probably won't say anything to anyone else. OK, cool — you're safe for now.

But what would happen if your thing got out to 50 people, or 200, or maybe the whole school found out what your thing was? That thing that you had been trying to keep to yourself this whole time is now public knowledge — and everyone you know (and even people you don't) — knows your secret. Even teachers and parents and other people in your community have heard about it. And not only do they all know, it got posted to Instagram and people have been commenting on it. A lot. Every day for the past week. And they haven't been saying very nice things. Someone even commented, "Yo, you should just kill yaself, lol." And you've been reading every comment, seeing every emoji and meme.

Now you're super stressed out. You haven't slept much that week because every time you walk down the hallways at school, people are looking at you and whispering to each other. Or pointing at you and laughing. You don't feel like you can talk to anyone because you feel humiliated that everyone knows your secret. What do you do now???

You don't have to add to the noise.

When someone tells you something in confidence, keep it. You don't have to rush to post it because you got that "piping hot tea" and you can't wait for all the likes and comments you're gonna get when everyone gets a sip. Think about how you might feel if someone did the same to you and make a different choice.

You don't have to add to the noise.

When you see something online about someone else that's negative, you don't have to comment. It's perfectly fine if you just keep scrolling. How would you feel if that person had been dealing with mean comments all day, then saw your comment, and that was the one that sent them over the edge? How would it make you feel to know that your comment was the last comment that someone saw?

You don't have to add to the noise.

You shouldn't forward negative things about other people either. Someone might be able to handle it if only three or four people see a mean post, but every time it gets forwarded, the potential number of people who might see it grows exponentially. Don't be the reason that negative info about someone goes viral.

You don't have to add to the noise.

No one is asking you to be a hero. If you wanted to say something nice about the person being bullied or let people know that it wasn't cool to say negative things about people, that would be awesome. However, it would be understandable if you didn't want to put yourself out there like that. But you know what you could do? You could report any posts you see that are bullying someone to the social media platform that they're posted on. You can do that anonymously. And the more you do it, and the more other people you can get to do it the better. You might be able to get the post taken down or even get the account removed.

Or you know what else you could do? You could do nothing.

YOU. DON'T. HAVE. TO. ADD. TO. THE. NOISE.

*If you are having suicidal thoughts, there is help available. You can call the National Suicide Prevention Lifeline at 1-800-273-8255.

ACTIVITY

Have you had a situation at your school or job where negative information about you or someone else was spread online?

What happened to you / that person?

_____
_____
_____
_____
_____
_____
_____
_____

How did you feel / how do you think that person felt?

_____
_____
_____
_____
_____
_____

Why do you think people spread info like this?

_____
_____
_____
_____
_____
_____
_____
_____

What should happen to people who spread negative info about people online?

_____
_____
_____
_____
_____
_____
_____
_____
_____
_____
_____

ACTIVITY

What are some ways that you as a student (or you as a group of students) could combat cyber bullying online?

Sexting

I can already see some of your eyes rolling, but yes, we're going to talk about sexting. Sexting is when you electronically send sexually explicit imagery to someone or when they electronically send sexually explicit imagery to you. Any time someone slides into your DMs and says "send nudes" and you do, you are sexting. So sexting can take place via social media, text message, email or any other internet-connected or cellular-connected method. And if you're minor, depending on where you live, sexting can still get you into a lot of trouble. Before we go any further, let me say that this section is NOT intended to shame anyone for sharing photos of themselves. I totally get that this is the way that a lot of people choose to express their affection or flirt with each other. At this point, it might seem like a normal thing to do because everyone you know is doing it. However, you have to understand that while this might be "just the way it is these days" not everyone sees it that way. And if you're under 18, you might still be facing some serious consequences depending on the laws where you live. My only motivation is to make sure that you have all the information you need to make the best decision for you.

In 2016, a 16-year-old girl in Maryland sent a sexually explicit video of herself to two friends. A few months later one of the friends shared the video not only with the entire student body of the school they both attended, but also with the school resource officer. Because of the way the laws in the state of Maryland are currently written, the school resource officer was required to share the video with the state prosecutor. The young woman who initially shared the video was charged with "illegally distributing child pornography" and "displaying an obscene item to a minor." She ended up being sentenced to supervised probation and electronic monitoring. That meant that she had to regularly report to a probation officer and allow them to visit her home. She also had to take an anger management course, submit to weekly drug testing, and get permission from her probation officer before she could leave the state. Fortunately, because she was a minor, she was not required to register as sex offender. Just last year in 2019, the Maryland Court of Appeals upheld the decision and her punishment.

There are quite a few things that are unfair about this story, not the least being that the student that shared her video in the first place was not disciplined in any way. However, no matter how you might feel about whether the punishment fit the crime, the law is the law. And unfortunately, the laws haven't yet caught up to the way we use our phones these days and they are different in each state. But no matter what state you live in, when it comes to minors and sexting, one fact remains true:

Sexually explicit imagery of a minor is child pornography.

This is not up for debate. The state you live in might not treat you as harshly as you would be treated somewhere else, but this is the simple truth. If you are a minor and you send a nude of yourself to someone else, you've exploited yourself and distributed child pornography. The person you send the pics to is now in possession of child pornography. And if they forward the pics to anyone else, they are now guilty of distribution as well. And while you may or may not face any penalties in your state depending on the laws there, federal law does not make any type of distinction as it relates to child pornography. If you're a minor who sends a photo or receives one, you can be prosecuted under federal law as an adult. One example of when federal law may intervene over state law is if you email someone a photo in a different state. Because the explicit imagery crossed state lines, you could be prosecuted under federal jurisdiction.

Some state governments understand that young people don't always make the best decisions, so the penalties for sexting are minor. You might have to pay a fine or complete an internet safety class or some other type of deterrent program. However, some states still treat each case as a felony — regardless of the age of the person involved. That could mean heavy fines, potential jail time, and the possibility that your name could end up on a sex offender registry. Whether or not you get prosecuted isn't up to you — something you thought wasn't a big deal might be a huge deal to someone else. Schools may be required by law to

SECTION TWO

report an incident if a teacher finds out. Or at a minimum, someone's dad might get angry that you have a nude picture of their daughter on your phone and decide to press charges. And once you're in front of a judge, your punishment is up to their discretion. They may be understanding of your young age and decide to take it easy on you — or they may decide to make an example of you and give you the harshest penalty possible. The point is you don't know whether the chips will fall in your favor or not.

ACTIVITY

Let's do some research. First, find out the sexting laws for minors in your state.

What are the different levels of penalties for different offenses?

_____
_____
_____
_____
_____
_____
_____
_____

Next, research what happens when your name is added to a sex offender registry?

_____
_____
_____
_____
_____
_____
_____
_____

SECTION TWO | ACTIVITY

What things are you no longer allowed to do?

_____
_____
_____
_____
_____
_____
_____
_____

How long could your name be on a sex offender list?

_____
_____
_____
_____

How would it change your life if you were added to a sex offender registry?

_____
_____
_____
_____
_____
_____
_____
_____
_____
_____

Revenge Porn

Image-based sexual abuse — or "revenge porn" — is a form of cyber-harassment or bullying that involves publicly posting an intimate image that the victim has not consented to have shared. Revenge porn can become an extreme consequence of sexting where the person in possession of nude pictures uploads those pictures to a pornographic site or uses the pictures to extort the sender. That extortion can come in the form of asking for more explicit photos or even blackmailing the sender for money. A lot of these situations start as relationships where two people are sharing explicit pictures with each other. Then, when the relationship is over, one of the people involved decides to retaliate against the other by posting the pictures online or sharing them with other people. Sometimes, the pictures can be sent to family members or employers to try to embarrass the sender. Or, if the pictures make it onto a pornographic site, that could lead to harassment from strangers as well. But it's not just people in relationships that can become the victims of revenge porn. If your phone gets hacked and someone shares private images without your consent or if you didn't even know the pictures were being taken — like for instance with a hidden camera in a locker room — those can also be considered revenge porn too.

There are 46 states that have laws dealing with revenge porn. The problem is this: The laws are different for each state, and they may not effectively address the offense. So depending on where you live, you could end up like the woman in California who in April 2018 was awarded $6.4 million dollars in a settlement against her boyfriend who shared intimate photos of her online. Or you could end up like a woman in New York who was arrested in November 2019 for uploading videos of her ex-boyfriend to Facebook. Women or men can be the victims or the perpetrators of revenge porn, and both can be prosecuted for it.

But even if you're able to get someone arrested or win a criminal or civil court case, the effects of revenge porn can go on for years and years. Victims of revenge porn have spent tens of thousands of dollars paying attorneys to try to get photos taken down from different websites online. And you may never be able to rid the internet of all the photos that might be out there. There will always be the possibility that a simple Google search will reveal pictures taken and shared years before. Beyond the financial expense, the psychological effects of revenge porn can be devastating. Victims of revenge porn have suffered from PTSD (post-traumatic stress disorder), anxiety and depression. One study of revenge porn victims revealed that over half the members of the study had considered suicide.

Revenge porn can be an extremely traumatic and isolating experience. It may truly feel like the end of the world because of the negative effects it can cause in a lot of different areas of your life. If you've been a victim of revenge porn, the most important thing to understand is that **it is not your fault**. The person who shared your photo without your consent is 100% responsible for their own behavior. One of the organizations created to fight revenge porn is the Cyber Civil Rights Initiative (www.cybercivilrights.org). They provide legal guidance and other resources to victims and they lobby governments to try to get laws created that will more effectively deal with the problem. It is also a good idea to talk to someone like a therapist if this has happened to you. Understanding that you're not alone and that there are people that truly want to help you can go a long way toward healing.

ACTIVITY

If you or someone you know has been the victim of revenge porn, please get help!

There are people and organizations out there that want to help you figure out what to do next and what your options are. Please don't suffer in silence!

How would you feel if you were a victim of revenge porn?

_____
_____
_____
_____
_____
_____
_____
_____
_____
_____
_____
_____
_____
_____

How might it affect the rest of your life in the future (i.e., school, jobs, dating, etc.)?

_____
_____
_____
_____
_____
_____

Let's do some research: In addition to the Cyber Civil Rights Initiative, what other organizations are out there to help fight revenge porn?

_____
_____
_____
_____
_____
_____

Are there any specific revenge porn laws in your state? Are they different from the sexting laws?

_____
_____
_____
_____
_____
_____

SECTION THREE

How to Make Sure Your Digital Footprint Is on the Right Path

Because I don't want you to think that being online is only gloom and doom, this final section of the book will help you make sure that you are representing yourself online in the best way possible. The internet is a very powerful tool — people make money online, causes are started, communities are built, and people are connected in ways that were never possible before. Sure, there are potential negative consequences but there are also some very positive things that you can accomplish online too. As long as you remember that everything you do online is a part of your digital footprint that then becomes a part of your personal brand, you can make decisions that will work in your favor.

Let's think back to the branding questions we talked about in Section One. When we talked about company brands, we mentioned logos, colors and all the physical ways a brand could be represented. Even when we talked about your personal brand, the way you presented yourself in person was a big part of it. This is all related to the way that you present your personal brand online too. Here are a couple of things to think about when you're representing your personal brand on social media platforms:

- **Username** — What is your username on the different social networks? Is it something that others might find offensive? Does it include obscene language or slurs? How would you explain the meaning of your username to someone else? How does your username reflect who you are and your personal brand? Your username is important because it's usually one of the first impressions that someone has of you online. When schools, potential employers and others search for you, your username is the first thing they have to make a determination about what kind of person they think you are. A lot of companies will follow you on social media before they hire you (remember Emily Clow?) or they might ask you to post on their behalf from your accounts once you become an employee. If you're posting company info from an account with a questionable username and someone sees it and complains to the company, your personal brand has now come into conflict with the company brand.

Ideally, you should be looking to claim your own given name as your username across multiple accounts. If you have a relatively common name this might be tricky, but you can add your middle initial or some other identifier to make it unique. The goal should be to have the same username across as many social platforms as possible. Even if your username isn't your legal name, it should still reflect your brand and you should try to have the same one on different platforms. My name is Stephanie Humphrey, but my brand is TechLifeSteph. And you can find me @TechLifeSteph on Instagram, Twitter, LinkedIn, Facebook, Snapchat and TikTok. Any good marketer will tell you that brand consistency is super important. The Nike brand is represented by @nike on all social media platforms across the board so that you'll always know exactly how to find them and so there won't be any confusion with another brand. Your personal brand is just as important as Nike's brand, right? Right! So make sure you start your brand on the right foot (pun intended) with a username that lets people know exactly who you are.

▸ **Profile photo** — Your profile photo is equally as important as your username because it's also a part of that first impression that people get when they search for you online. A profile photo can make or break a potential opportunity to connect with someone. I've turned down many a friend/follow request because the person in the profile photo had a middle finger up or their profile photo was a logo or image of something I didn't agree with. The profile photo you use can say a lot about the type of content someone can expect to find on your page. I have a personal brand that I am building and trying to protect just like you do. So if there is something about your brand that might be offensive to me, that creates a conflict with my own brand that I don't want to have. And if I'm already seeing something questionable in your profile photo, I won't even bother to consider what the rest of your feed might look like. While I can't necessarily control everyone that follows me, I can certainly control who I follow. Is it fair? Maybe, maybe not. Does it happen all the time? Absolutely! Think back to Emily Clow. If she were actually working on a career as a bikini model, it would make perfect sense that her profile picture and a lot of the content on her feed would be of her in bikinis. And although she was well within her rights to post whatever pictures she wanted, she also has to consider what that says about her personal brand. No one knows how great a marketer she could have been because that wasn't what she chose to show on her feeds. Like the old saying goes, a picture really is worth a thousand words and your profile picture can speak loudly before you ever get the chance to say anything. One more thing about profile photos — not having one may be just as damaging to your brand as having the wrong picture. If you don't have a profile pic, people may think that your account is fake. You might not necessarily like the way you look in pictures, but it's still important to have one included in your profile. We'll talk a little bit more about profile pictures when we get to the discussion on LinkedIn.

▸ **Bio** — Following the same logic as with your username and profile picture, your bio is one of the most effective ways to promote your personal brand. You might not have many characters available to use, but you can give people a good idea of who you are and what is important to you from your bio. As an example, here's my Instagram bio:

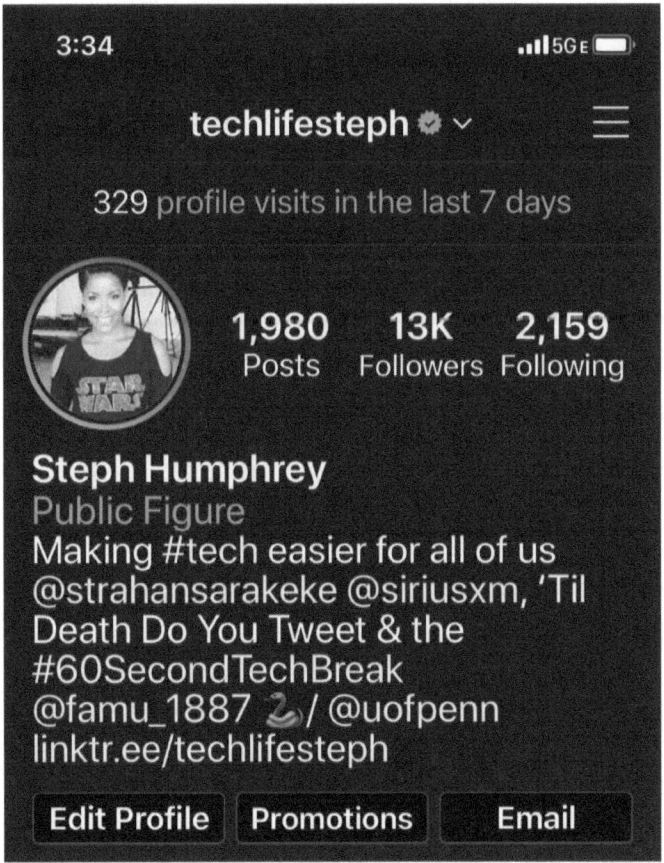

First, you can see that my username is consistent with my brand, and my profile photo showcases my personality in a positive way — unless you're a fan of Star Trek instead of Star Wars! Now take a look at my bio. The first line tells you exactly what I do — "Making #tech easier for all of us." That's literally my personal brand in seven words — I help people understand how technology makes our lives easier. The next three lines of my bio tell you where I do that, whether it's on television, on the radio, online with my #60SecondTechBreak or in person with 'Til Death Do You Tweet. The next line promotes my education as a graduate of Florida A&M University and the University of Pennsylvania. I use my education to connect with other alumni, so I wanted to make sure that it was highlighted in my bio. The last line of my bio is a link that will take you to my website, YouTube channel, merch store and other information about me online. That's a lot of information in just six short lines of text! From those six lines, you know exactly what I do and where I do it, where I went to school to learn about how to do it and how you can get more information about what I do.

An easy way to come up with a bio that represents your personal brand well is to think about your "elevator pitch." It only takes a few seconds when you're in an elevator going from the first floor of a building to, say the 10th floor. Imagine if someone got on the elevator with you who could snap their fingers and make your wildest dream for yourself come true. Not that dream where you win a million dollars and buy a Bentley. That other dream where you want to be just like LeBron James or Michelle Obama or Mark Zuckerberg when you grow up. That dream that you've been working for your whole life. That dream that makes you study harder or practice harder every day. That dream you have where you think "if I just had a chance to show the right person how awesome I am, I know I could crush it!" If the right person could see how beautifully you sing or how sick your jumper was or could invest money in your million-dollar business idea, you would be set for life.

If the person on the elevator could make that dream happen, what would you say to them? How would you convince them to give you a chance? Remember, you only have those few seconds between the first floor and the 10th floor. That's not a lot of time at all, so you have to make it quick and you have to make it good. How you tell someone about who you are, what you do and what your dreams are in 15-30 seconds is your elevator pitch. You have to be brief and succinct, but you still have to convey a fair amount of information to someone to get them to listen to you. It's a good place to start on social media too because the bio field on most platforms are limited by a specific number of characters. What are those 180 characters going to say about your personal brand?

Another thing you'll notice in my bio are the use of hashtags. Hashtags are not just phrases with a "#" in front of them that make your posts seem clever. They also make your content searchable. So if someone happens to be looking for tech accounts on IG, my page will be in those search results. And if someone wants to check out the content that I create, I can just tell them to put #60SecondTechBreak in the search bar and all my videos will be returned in the search. Think about what hashtags you can use in your bio to further enhance your personal brand. If you play a sport or an instrument or if you're passionate about a cause, make sure you let people know by including it in your bio and using a hashtag. Keep in mind though, that you don't want to overdo it. Every word in your bio doesn't need to be a hashtag. The key is to use them strategically for the words you add to your bio that people tend to search for most often. Or you can use hashtags for words or phrases that aren't necessarily common, but that you want to become associated with your brand in particular (like #60SecondTechBreak). The more you can do to establish and develop your personal brand online the better.

ACTIVITY

What is your elevator pitch?

Take some time to think about it and write it down. You may even want to memorize it. Even if you don't use it in your bio, it's still a good thing to have because it helps you be clear about who you are and what you want out of life. And, you never know who you'll meet in an elevator...

_____
_____
_____
_____
_____
_____
_____
_____
_____
_____
_____
_____
_____
_____
_____
_____
_____
_____

ACTIVITY

Now it's time to audit your social media accounts.

What do the usernames, profile photos and bios of each platform you're on reflect about your personal brand?

_____
_____
_____
_____
_____
_____
_____
_____
_____
_____
_____
_____

Does anything need to change to be more consistent or to represent your brand in a more positive way?

_____
_____
_____
_____

SECTION THREE | ACTIVITY

Are you using hashtags strategically to make your accounts discoverable?

Remember the conversation we had about search engine optimization (SEO) in Section One? Once you've gotten your username, profile pics and bios together, think about doing a little extra to use SEO to your advantage. Here are a few easy SEO tips to think about:

- ▶ If you are not on any social networks, think about getting "social" — **IF it's OK with your parents**. You don't have to try to be on every platform at once, but establishing a presence somewhere is a great way to begin building an online brand.
- ▶ What's in a name? Try to use the same username consistently across all your online platforms. If you're John Smith one place and John M. Smith somewhere else, it can not only confuse someone searching for you, but also lower your overall search ranking too. Using a middle initial or some other qualifier may help if you have a common name, but the key is to use it uniformly across the web.
- ▶ This is worth repeating: If you are on a social network(s), make sure your profile is complete. That means profile picture, bio, location, etc. This helps when someone searches for you and finds a link to one of your social profiles — if they're complete, people are more likely to interact with them (you) and there is less of a chance of confusing you for someone else.
- ▶ Include links in your social profiles. If you have a website/blog, YouTube channel, articles that you've written/contrib-

uted to on other websites, etc., make sure to include some of those in your social media bios.

▸ Create content. Start a website/blog/vlog, YouTube channel, Medium account, podcast or About.me page. Write an article for your school paper. All those sources linked together create a solid SEO foundation.

▸ If you do nothing else, PLEASE check your spelling and grammar! You can totally sink your personal SEO with simple errors that can make you practically invisible online. That college recruiter or potential employer might not have reached out to you because they were searching for a "manager," not a "manger." Always proofread your headlines, bios, etc., carefully.

▸ There are different areas on a page that rank higher in search indexing than others, like the URL of a page, a title or headline and tags. If you can include your name and/or a keyword or two in these areas, it will help boost your SEO.

▸ Be consistent. When your social media accounts or website become less active, they fall further down the page in a search result. And while you don't need to be posting something every minute of every day, you do need to decide how much you are able to do and then commit to it. However, keep in mind that committing to posting once a month may not help your SEO as much as you'd like. If you're pressed for time, take advantage of scheduling tools like Buffer or Hootsuite to help with the challenge of maintaining regular posting.

Getting Started on LinkedIn

Depending on who is reading this book and how old you are, this next section might not make that much sense to you right now. But if you are a high school student or older, it is absolutely NOT too early to create a LinkedIn page. With over 600 million total users, 260 million monthly active users and two new people signing up every second, LinkedIn is the world's largest professional social network. And if you aspire to be a working professional in any industry, your digital footprint should include an account on this site. Think of LinkedIn as your digital resume, but also as a digital marketplace where you can connect with other people and grow your personal brand. A Pew research study from 2018 showed that only 9% of high school students have a profile on LinkedIn — so this is an awesome way for you to stand out! Including your LinkedIn page on a college application will set you apart from your peers and show people that you are serious about your personal brand and your future place in the workforce.

Setting yourself up on LinkedIn is critical because you don't want to wait until you need to connect with someone to connect with someone. In other words, establishing your network in advance will save you a lot of headache later on. A lot of high schools now require internships for graduation, college recruiters are on LinkedIn, or you might be entering the workforce straight from high school. No matter what your future plans are, you'll need a network of other people to accomplish your goals. Connecting with people on LinkedIn lets you start to grow that network and engage and interact with that network before you need to reach out to them for something. You don't want to wait until the week before your internship is supposed to start to try to connect with a potential employer on LinkedIn to find one. It doesn't work like that.

Think about the last person that asked you for something — maybe for a ride somewhere or to borrow money. How well did you know the person asking? If it was a family member you probably didn't hesitate to do the favor. You probably wouldn't hesitate if it was one of your best friends either. Even if it was someone you didn't interact with every day, but knew to be trustworthy, you might consider doing a favor for them too. But what if a total stranger walked up to you and asked to borrow your phone? Would you just hand it over to them? Even if they looked respectable and promised you, they only needed to make a quick phone call, would you do it? I don't know about you, but unless it's an emergency, it's not likely that I'm handing my thousand-dollar device to someone I've never met before. That's what it feels like when you reach out to people on LinkedIn you don't know to ask for a job, an introduction to someone else or anything. You haven't taken the time to develop a relationship with someone, yet you want them to advocate for you — do you a favor — just based on the strength of your profile. While there's always the chance that your personal brand is represented so well that someone jumps at the opportunity to connect with you based on your reputation alone, there's a much better chance that your request will be ignored completely. LinkedIn is about making and growing connections, providing value for others first, then using that network to help you achieve your goals. So let's get you set up so you can start connecting!

Are You an All-Star?

Once you get an account created on LinkedIn, you'll want to work toward becoming an "All-Star." That designation is not there for you to brag about how awesome you are — it signifies that your profile is complete. There are different levels of profile completeness on LinkedIn (Beginner, Intermediate, Advanced, Expert, All-Star), and there are things you are required to include in your profile to reach each level. We're going to focus on getting you to All-Star status for one very good reason: according to LinkedIn, users with complete profiles are **40 times** more likely to receive opportunities through the site. That could be a huge potential missed opportunity because of something that is relatively simple to do. I totally understand that you may not be able to complete some of the areas of your profile because there are things you just haven't done yet in life, but we're going to do the best we can with what you do have — which is still a lot! There are seven criteria LinkedIn requires to consider your profile complete — so let's go through them and help you become an All-Star!

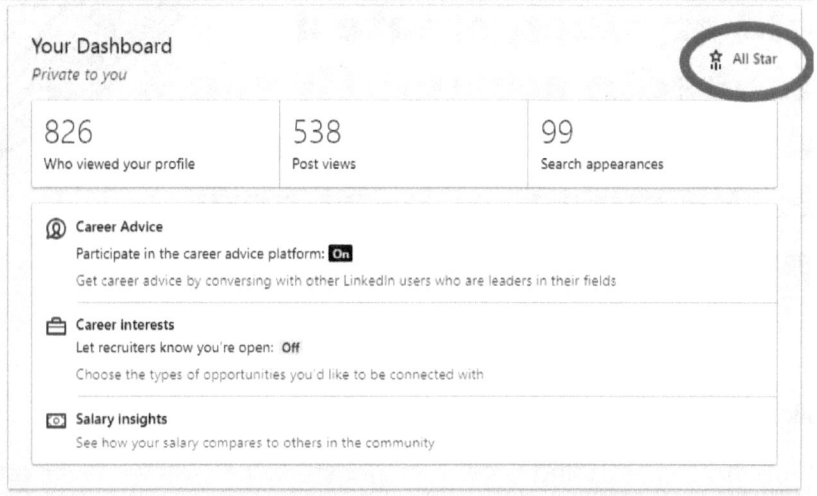

ACTIVITY

If you are 15 years old or older, create a LinkedIn account (if you don't already have one). Make sure you have your parent's permission.

A Note About the "Add Profile Section"

One more quick thing before we get started. If you've never set up a LinkedIn profile before, some of the sections will already be visible to you and waiting for your input. You can always click the "+" in the upper right corner of the box to add more content to any section or the pencil icon to edit the content in any section. While you're completing your profile, pay attention to the "Add profile section" drop-down menu in the upper right corner of your profile page. When you click on that, you'll see all the possible sections you can add to your profile. There's a cool feature included when you click on the arrow to expand the section list — you get an audit of that section. For example, if your "Intro" section is complete, you'll see a message under that heading that says so. If it's not, you'll get a suggestion of what you can do to complete the section.

The "Featured" section is where you can highlight something specific that you want people to see right away. You can add photos, videos, links or other media here. The "Featured" section appears right under your "Intro" and "About" sections, so it will be one of the first things people see when they view your profile. This is where you want to put your best stuff! Don't overdo it, but if you have an award you're proud of or a video of some of your latest work, this is where you get to show it off.

The "Background" section is where your work experience, education and lots of other information will be found, so make sure you check it out — I'll be referring to information in this section later in the book.

You don't have to complete all the sections suggested under the "Add profile section" menu for your profile to be an "All-Star," but it's a good guide for what you could add to make your profile shine. Your LinkedIn profile will continue to evolve and change as your experiences change. It's a tool that can help you grow your personal brand, and we want to make sure we're using it as effectively as possible, but don't feel pressure to try to make it look "perfect."

Profile Picture

I am of the belief that including a picture is one of the most important — if not THE most important — parts of your LinkedIn profile. Statistics show that having a photo means your profile is **21 times** more likely to be viewed. I can tell you personally that it is extremely rare for me to accept an invitation to connect from a profile that doesn't have a photo. If I don't already know the person in real life, my first assumption is that the profile could be fake. Recruiters and other potential business contacts may make the same guess, or they could think that you're not up to date on technology and couldn't figure out how to upload a picture. In the workshops I do for adult professionals with TDDYT Pro, I've heard concern expressed about the possibility of potential recruiters/business prospects using profile pictures to discriminate against you based on race or perceived age. Discrimination in hiring is a reality that our society has not figured out how to eradicate yet, if ever. However, I would maintain that not having a picture is still more damaging to your profile than including one. It can be challenging for someone to connect with all your accomplishments when they can't "see" you — some may even think you have something to hide. You also want to take advantage of the idea that there are companies out there that are actually looking for diversity. And since we're talking about using LinkedIn as a personal brand-building tool in addition to any job search activities, does it make sense that anyone would take the personal brand of someone they can't see seriously? For better or worse, a big part of your personal brand is how you look. First impressions still matter. I am convinced that you will miss out on far more opportunities because of a missing profile picture than any discrimination you might face from having one posted.

A professional headshot is the best option, but you don't necessarily need to spend money to hire a photographer. Most newer smartphones take very high-quality pictures. Make sure you're somewhere well-lit (with the light source facing you) in front of a solid background and shoot from the chest up. And while you don't have to show a full set of teeth, you want to look friendly and approachable. This isn't the time to post your best selfie or vacation photo from the beach. And make sure your photo is up to date. You might be new to the LinkedIn platform, but you don't want to upload a picture that is more than 2-3 years old. There may be some cases where your picture can be something that highlights your business if you've already started one, but I'd still recommend the profile photo be a picture of you. You can use the cover photo to showcase your business or anything else about your personal brand you'd want someone to know.

Lastly, I'd say that while these are good tips for your LinkedIn profile photo, you don't have to be so buttoned up with the rest of your social networks. We talked about this a little bit in a previous section. The picture I use in my LinkedIn profile is different than the one I use on Instagram, but they both still positively reflect my personal brand. You're allowed to have a little fun with your photo, but you should think about what each social network is typically used for and what type of content you intend to post. If your TikTok account is where you post your #dancechallenges, the profile pic can be something that reflects that — like maybe you mid-Renegade!

ACTIVITY

If you haven't already, upload a profile photo to your LinkedIn account.

Also, create and upload a cover photo that reflects your brand.

You can use any tool you want, but Canva is a free resource where you can create cover photos for social media that are already formatted for each platform.

Headline

The headline is the area under your photo and name where you list your job title (or in your case, it might be the job or internship you're interested in), but it's a lot more than that as well. This is where you get to tell the world who you are and what you have to offer. The headline is also how you will be searched for on the platform. That means that what you have (or don't have) included in your headline can mean a missed opportunity because a recruiter or business prospect couldn't find you. You get a limit of 120 characters for this section if you edit your profile using the web version of the LinkedIn. However, if you're editing using the

LinkedIn app, you get additional characters. I'm not sure if this is simply the company trying to drive more app use, but as of the writing of this book that option was available. Either way, it's still not a ton of space, so use all the characters you have available to you and use them wisely. And remember, the goal of the headline is to be succinct, so don't use the mobile hack as an opportunity to write your life's dissertation. What you also don't want to do is simply use the headline that LinkedIn auto-generates for you. Your job title and company name are a decent start, but that shouldn't be the only thing reflecting your personal brand in this section.

 I want to take a minute right now to talk briefly about keywords. Remember the conversation we had in Section One about Search Engine Optimization (SEO)? The idea was that you had some control over your online narrative because you used digital platforms that took advantage of really good SEO. One of the things that makes a digital platform have good SEO is the use of keywords on that site. Keywords are those words and phrases that are most often searched for online for any subject. When you start typing something in a Google search box, the words and phrases Google uses to try to autocomplete what you type are the most popular keywords for that particular search. In other words, those phrases are the way that people search most often for that information. And you can use keywords in your profile to maximize the SEO on LinkedIn too. When recruiters or potential employees search for you on LinkedIn, they're using LinkedIn's search engine, just like you use Google's search engine. So SEO still matters because it's still what's going to move your profile to the top of the search results on that platform.

When you're creating your headline, you might want to think about what keywords best fit the objective you're trying to accomplish. If you were interested in coding, keywords like "software developer" would be good to put somewhere in your headline. You can use tools like wordtracker.com or moz.com to find commonly used keywords.

One word of caution though. Just like with hashtags, don't overdo it! Having too many keywords in a profile (or on your own website or blog) is known as "keyword stuffing." A lot of companies try to do it so that their websites will rank higher in search results. However, search engines like Google or LinkedIn know that people try to cheat the system, so they look out for it and will actually rank your profile lower in search results. Add a few keywords to your headline where they make sense but don't go overboard.

Most of the better LinkedIn headlines I've seen either highlight skills, accomplishments or value — and if you can find a way to include all three you've hit the jackpot. A headline that emphasized skills might look something like this:

Jane Doe | Front-End Developer | Future Full-stack Engineer |HTML5, Python, CSS3, PHP

Anyone viewing this profile will get an immediate and fairly comprehensive list of this person's skillset. And potential recruiters will likely be searching for candidates using some of these terms, so this profile will be higher on the list of search results. You'll also notice the second title — "Future Full-stack Engineer." As a student, it's perfectly OK to add a position that you aspire to in your headline.

An accomplishment-based headline might read like this:

John Doe | Emmy award-winning Producer, NYT Best-selling Author & Writing Coach

If I had an Emmy, I'd certainly lead with it in my profile! Awards and recognition can lend authority and prestige to your personal brand, but you want to be careful to avoid superlatives that can sound like bragging. For example, instead of declaring yourself a "Top-performing student," you should have the numbers and/or recognition to back up that claim. A better headline would read *"Duncan High School Valedictorian, Student Council President and Future Software Developer."*

Now let's take a look at a headline that emphasizes value:

This is my real LinkedIn profile headline. It tells you what I do — contribute tech content to various properties of ABC News. But it also tells you how I add value — helping people with technology and digital citizenship. The term "public speaker" is a very common keyword, so I wanted to make sure I included it so that my profile was as visible as possible. I also threw a hashtag in there for more branding of my original content. I used the mobile app hack to add more characters because I wanted to highlight not only where I worked, but the content that I create on my own as well. My goal was to try to be as succinct as possible while giving the viewer enough information to make them want to keep reading the rest of my profile. How'd I do?

Ultimately, you want your headline to reflect your personal brand while also being tailored to your audience. It should help people understand who you are and how you add value. And it should include keywords and hashtags to make your headline searchable.

ACTIVITY

Create a headline that highlights either skills, accomplishments or value — or some combination of the three — and add it to your profile.

Industry / Location

Your industry and location information are included after your headline. You might not necessarily have an industry right now and that's OK. Think about the industry where you see yourself in the future — maybe it's technology, media or something else. This field won't be visible to others in your profile, but it is searchable, so you want to make sure potential contacts have every option available to find you. When you click on the pencil in the right corner to edit the intro, you'll see fields in the pop-up box for industry and location. If you are actively job searching now and you want to relocate or you'll be going to school in a different city, I've read advice that suggests you make your location that of the place where you'd like to be as opposed to where you live right now. Some recruiters do filter search results by geographical area, so you might potentially be missing out on a dream opportunity if they can't find you based on this field. Location information is also an important keyword too. Ideally, you want to make sure all the fields in the "Intro" section of your profile are complete.

ACTIVITY
Add your industry and location to your profile.

Summary

The summary comes after the headline (it's the "About" section), and this is a good place to let people get to know the real you. It's where you get to explain your headline in more detail and further establish your personal brand. You can include some notable achievements, like if your debate team won the citywide championship or you were awarded "Employee of the Month" for three months in a row at your after-school job. But you'll also set the foundation in your summary for your "WHY?" What are you passionate about? What is it about you that makes you unique from everyone else? It's where you can show people some of your school or job highlights and emphasize your strengths, but you don't want to include your entire resume.

It's recommended that your summary be authentic and conversational, so steer clear of referring to yourself in third person. That means you can write like you would normally speak. Instead of saying, "Stephanie is very passionate about artificial intelligence, and she finished in the top 10 of her school's robotics tournament," you can just say, "I'm passionate about robotics and was able to showcase my abilities in AI by placing in the top 10 of my school's annual tournament." You'll also want to include keywords/phrases here as well. You have a 2,000-character limit, so make sure you tell a story people will remember! Using smaller paragraphs and bulleted lists will make your accomplishments stand out. And while it's not required, there is an opportunity to add supporting media (links to website, YouTube, etc.) in your summary so take advantage of it if you can.

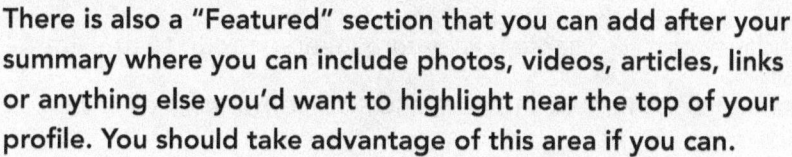

ACTIVITY

Come up with a killer summary, and add it to your profile.

There is also a "Featured" section that you can add after your summary where you can include photos, videos, articles, links or anything else you'd want to highlight near the top of your profile. You should take advantage of this area if you can.

Education

If you click the "Add profile section" under your headline, you'll see the option to add your education to the "Background" section. Keep in mind you're not required to include the dates you attended school if you think that might be detrimental — whether you're a new college grad who doesn't want a lack of experience to show or a more "seasoned" professional who thinks your graduation date will reveal too much experience. Even if you're in high school right now, you can (and should) still add that to your profile. As you're typing your school's name in that field, some names will show up in the autocomplete list, but others won't. That's OK — continue typing your school's name, add the rest of your information, and save that section. Don't forget to include vocational education here as well. The education section can also include things like coding bootcamps or online courses too. You can also add any school activities you think might be relevant in this section, such as fraternities/sororities, student government, sports teams, band or other school clubs. Keep in mind — your most recent education will show up in your intro with your name, headline, etc. To disable this feature, head back up to the "Intro" section, click the pencil to edit, and scroll down until you see this:

Uncheck the box labeled "Show education in my intro" and you're good to go! I don't necessarily recommend disabling this for high school or college students. Your education is a big part of your personal brand right now, and you want as many relevant points of connection showing in your profile as possible. If someone comes across your profile but only has time to skim the intro, the fact that you have a shared connection with them through the school you attend might make all the difference.

Also keep in mind — there is a separate section of your profile where you can list certifications and professional licenses, so you don't have to stuff the "Education" section with everything. However, having this section completed allows you to connect with other alumni and start building your network right away.

ACTIVITY
Complete the education section of your profile.

Experience

This section is the trickiest for students because your work experience might be limited, if you've had a job yet at all. But there are still some things you can add here. Any part-time or summer work should be included in this section. Even babysitting counts — that requires leadership, time management and a lot of other skills to do well. If you haven't had a paying job yet, I'd recommend using this section to talk about what responsibilities you do have. Here are a couple of screenshots illustrating what you could add to this section if you haven't had a job yet:

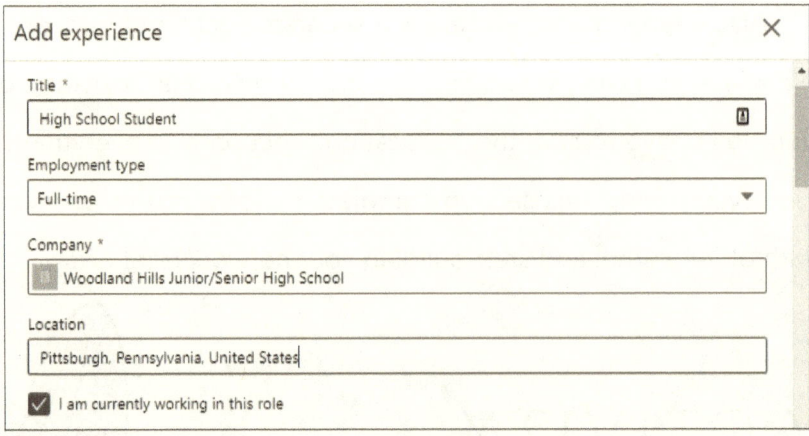

You can see the title and company reflect your current role and "place of employment." Having the box checked "I am currently working in this role" ensures you won't be left out of certain searches. Here's what a possible job description could look like:

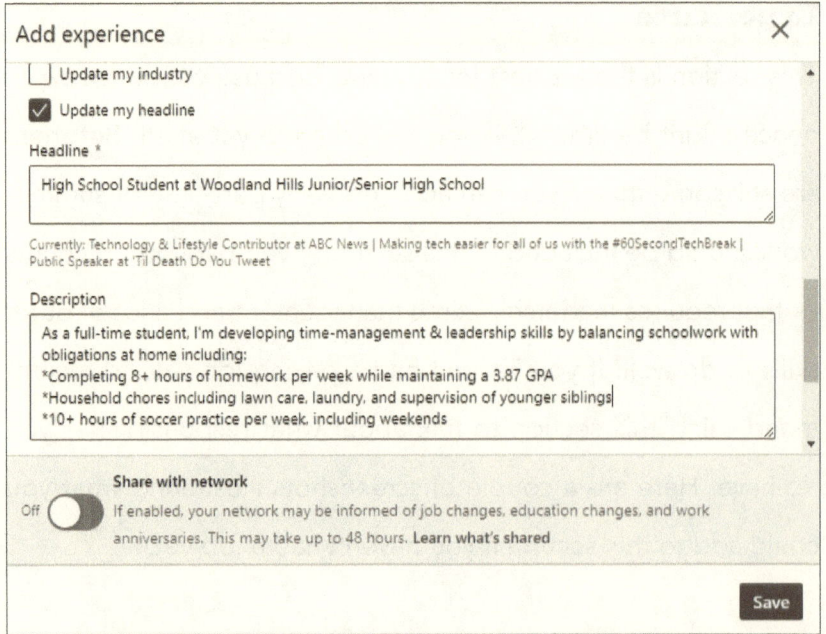

There are a few of things to pay attention to here, and we'll start with the "Description" field. Listing information with bullet points makes it easier to read, and this area will look a lot like a traditional resume to some degree. You notice that I've used numbers to quantify some accomplishments, like "completing 8+ hours of homework per week," "maintaining a 3.87 GPA," or "10+ hours of soccer practice per week." You want to be as specific as possible to verify your skillset. I've also used some keywords in my description, like "time-management" and "leadership."

The second thing you want to pay attention to is the "Headline" in this section. LinkedIn will automatically generate a generic headline for you based on the information in this part of your profile. That's usually not the most descriptive way to display your personal brand to the world. You can uncheck the box that says "Update my headline" and use the headline you came up with earlier in this book.

Also, check out the toggle switch at the bottom of the screenshot that says "Share with network." Having that turned on means that the people you're connected to on LinkedIn will get a notification every time you add a new job, have a job anniversary, add new education or any number of changes to your profile. Sometimes it's worthwhile to do, like if you move and want to let people know you're open to opportunities in a new area. But sometimes it can get overwhelming for other people's feeds, or there might just be times when you want to keep your life changes quiet. It's totally up to you, but think about what you and the people in your network stand to gain if this setting is enabled.

At the bottom of the experience section, you also have the option to add any supporting media or links in this section as well. So if you have videos of you on the job or samples of some of your work, make sure to add that too.

This might not apply to you, but the jury is still out on how many jobs you should have listed in this section. I've come across experts that say it should read like a traditional resume, with no employment gaps present and job listings practically as far back as you can remember. Some people have had this work to their benefit — you're always looking for a way to make a connection with someone on LinkedIn, and a job from 15 years ago might just do the trick. I've also spoken to recruiters and HR professionals that have said with the volume of inquiries they get on a daily basis, they most likely won't have the time to look past the first two to three listings anyway. LinkedIn only shows the first three to five entries of any section before you see the link to "See All," so you wouldn't necessarily be cluttering your profile if you decided to list more positions. My personal opinion is that anything you add to your profile should be relevant to your current personal brand. I haven't been an engineer for over a decade, but I believe my technical experience is relevant to what I do currently on television, so I kept it in my profile. You'll have to decide how much or how little you're comfortable sharing, but keeping your personal brand in mind and using relevancy to that brand as your criteria is a good place to start.

Quick Tip: if you are currently in between jobs, you should still have an entry with the "I am currently working in this role" box checked. That job listing could state that you're a student or that you're seeking a specific position, but you want to have something current included so that you don't get left out of certain search results.

ACTIVITY
Even if the only job you've ever had up to this point is "student," you still want to add something to this section.

Skills / Endorsements

In the "Skills" section, you're able to add different things to your profile that you're good at. They can be technical skills, such as using video editing software like Final Cut Pro. Or maybe you have some industry knowledge in video production or you're a great writer. You can even add interpersonal skills like public speaking to the list too. You'll need to add at least five skills to reach "All-Star" status on your profile. Click the "Add profile section" and then click the "+" button under the "Skills" section. I think it goes without saying that you should only be adding skills at which you have a legitimate proficiency — meaning things you can actually do! You can add up to 50 skills — and be sure to include any that are relevant to your objective and your personal brand.

If you are actively looking for a job, check out the skills that are most requested in the job postings that interest you and list those in your profile (but only if you have those skills!). As a working professional, keep in mind that "Microsoft Word" or other basic software knowledge is typically no longer considered a skill — employers expect you to have a fundamental understanding of heritage technology like this — so it's up to you whether to include it in this section. But as a student, I'd say that while you're looking to build your skillset, any software or other relevant experience is appropriate to add.

Choosing skills to add to your profile is a matter of search strategy too. The skills that you choose are then presented to your connections when it's time to endorse you. Endorsements are when your connections cosign the fact that you have a particular skill — they get the chance to say "yes" to the question of whether you are good at the thing you say you are. The more skills you list, the more spread out your endorsements may be which results in fewer endorsements per skill. This in turn can hurt your discoverability in search results. What might also happen is that you get more endorsements for lesser skills, which optimizes your search results for something you'd rather not emphasize as much. Make sure you're regularly reviewing your endorsements as well. Your connections get served endorsement requests, not only based on the skills you listed but also on related skills — or at least what the LinkedIn algorithm thinks is a related skill. That "related skill" may not turn out to be related at all, or it just may not be a skill that you would actually claim to have. I have had to delete endorsements from my profile in the past because they were for skills I wouldn't necessarily say I was proficient in, and you should do the same. Regular skill/endorsement audits of your profile ensure that all of the information listed is up to date and accurate — I know it sounds like a lot, but it's definitely worth it!

ACTIVITY
Add at least three skills to your profile. If it's appropriate, ask someone you know on LinkedIn to write you a recommendation.

Connections

The last thing you must have to complete your LinkedIn profile is at least 50 connections. In part, it shows that you are actively using the platform the way it was intended. Using the platform consistently also helps with SEO. Search for people you already know in real life, or search for people who share the same education or industry. If you have a mentor, coach or former teacher that you look up to you could start by connecting with them. If you do already have a job, it's up to you whether or not you want to connect with current or former coworkers — if you're using LinkedIn to actively look for a different job or if you're trying to start your side hustle, that might not be the best idea. One thing you do NOT want to do is spam everyone you know. LinkedIn has some options where you can send a connection request to everyone in your email contacts. Do not — I repeat — do not do this! It's unprofessional, and you've just given LinkedIn access to all of your contacts, which is a huge violation of their privacy. If you're setting up a new profile and LinkedIn asks you if you want to import your Gmail or Outlook contacts, just say no! It might take a little longer to reach out to people you already know, but it's still the better way to connect. However, no matter who you're trying to connect to, there is one thing that I believe you MUST do when reaching out: Personalize your invitation.

When you send an invitation to connect to someone, that

person will see a snippet of your profile in a list of invitations with an option to accept or deny the request. They'll see your photo (because I know you have one!), your headline and whether you have any connections in common. For me, if the headline is interesting enough, I may take the time to actually look at the full profile to see if we have enough in common for me to want to make a connection. But usually, I'm scrolling through a long list of invites from people I don't know and without some context, I'm probably going to keep scrolling or deny the request altogether. The better option is to personalize the invite. Personalizing lets you add a few words to the invite to let the other person know where they know you from or why you want to connect with them. It makes you look more professional and increases the likelihood that your connection request will be accepted. Personalizing an invite to connect works a little differently depending on whether you're using LinkedIn on a computer or a smartphone, so I've included some screenshots for each case below:

On a Computer:

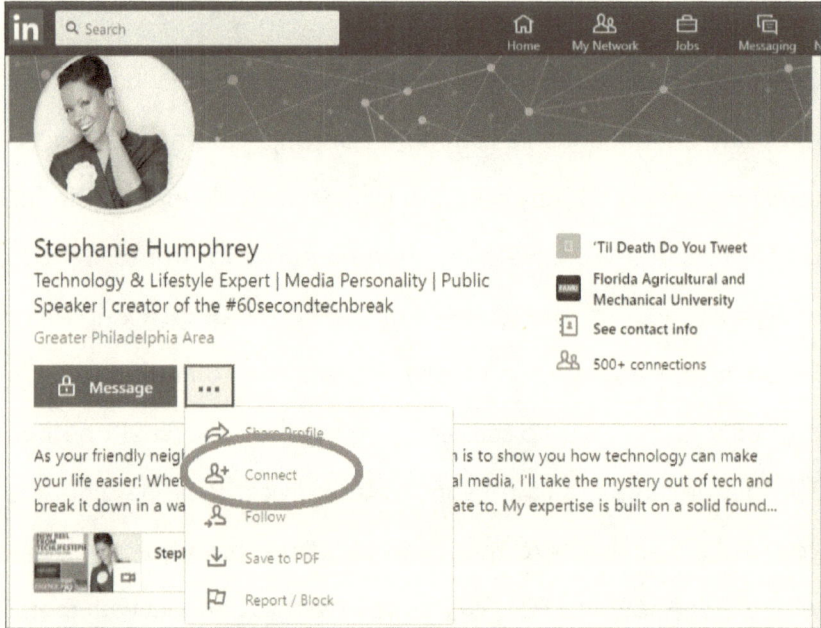

Depending on how a person's account privacy settings are set up, you may see different options to connect on their profile page. For example, in addition to the "Message" button, you might also see a "Connect" button on the page. If you only see a "Message" button, you want to click the "..." button. One note — instead of the button you see here, there may be a "More..." button displayed — that's what you'll click.

This is the next screen you'll see if you're sending a connection request on a computer. Click on the "Connect" option.

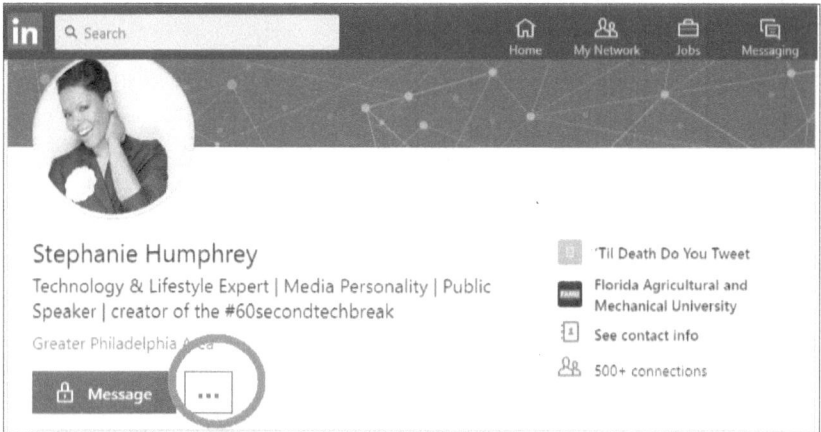

LinkedIn will then give you an option to customize the invitation — don't send a request without it! If the person you're trying to connect with does have a "Connect" button in their profile, just press it and the message above will pop up automatically.

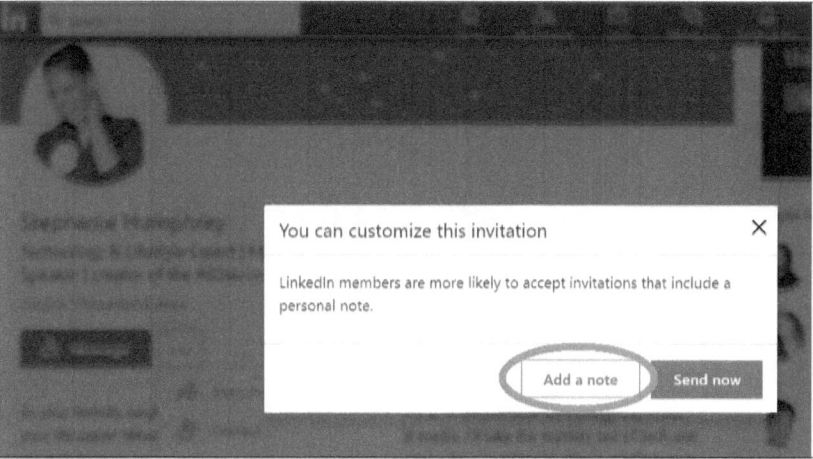

Once you've made it to the screen shown above, you can customize your invitation:

On a Smartphone:

On a smartphone, the profile screen of the person you want to connect with will look very similar to the web version. In this case, on a mobile device, no matter what other button options are available, you want to choose the option circled below. Keep in mind again that there may be a "More..." button instead of the one shown.

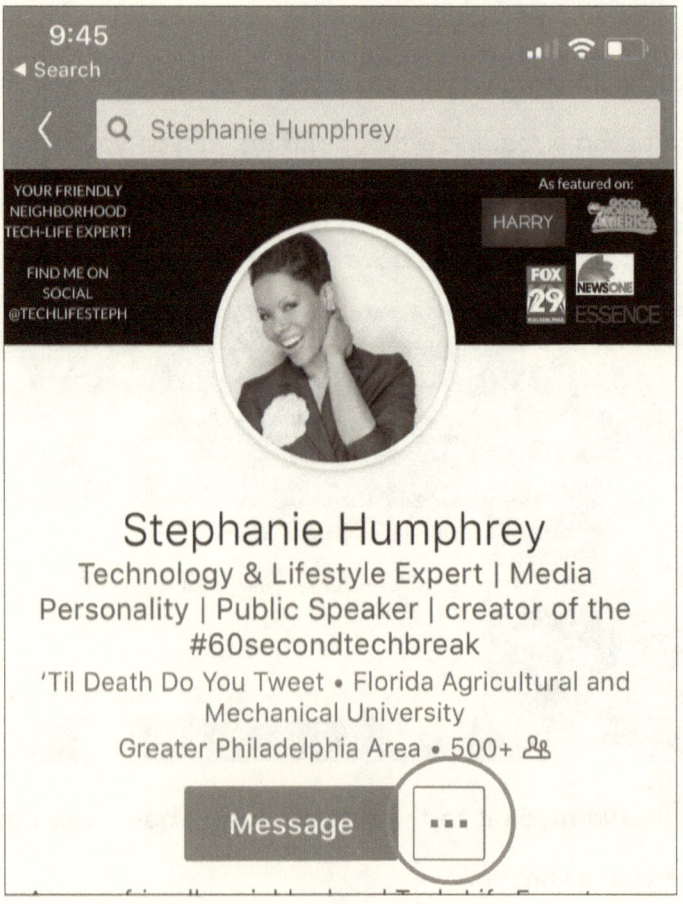

SECTION THREE

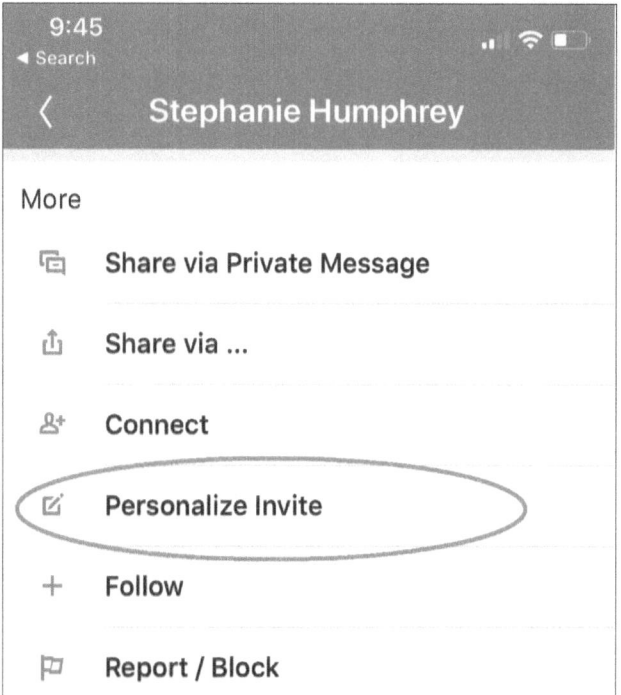

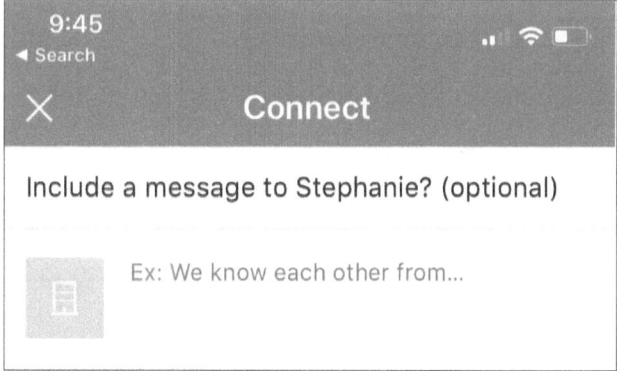

As you can see, your character limit is fairly small (300 characters max), but that's more than enough space to make a case for why someone would want to connect with you. You can mention where you met them, that it was nice to meet them and that you're following up. Or if you were referred to them by a mutual connection, talk about why that person thought you should reach out to them. If you don't know them at all, explain how connecting with you will add value for them. Maybe you read an article on them or saw one of their posts on social media (or on LinkedIn) and want to understand more about what they do. Make sure you reference the article or post or something else about them to show that you've done your research.

I wanted to take the time to explain the importance of connection etiquette because you should understand that LinkedIn isn't supposed to be used as a free-for-all where you send connection requests to any and everyone you come across. Even some of the suggestions LinkedIn makes of "people you may know" might not be appropriate. Quality over quantity is the name of the game on this platform. With that in mind, you also aren't obligated to accept every connection request you get either. Use LinkedIn as a tool to identify those people who can have a positive impact on your personal brand and future career by being strategic about whom you connect with.

ACTIVITY

Think about someone you'd want to connect with on LinkedIn.

Then come up with a personalized connection request, and if their privacy settings permit, send it to them. Good luck!

_____
_____
_____
_____
_____
_____
_____
_____
_____
_____
_____
_____
_____
_____
_____
_____
_____
_____
_____
_____

Other LinkedIn Profile Add-ons:

All the above sections are the minimum criteria you need to complete your LinkedIn profile and get to "All-Star" status, but there is a lot of other information you can (and should) add as well. If you head to the "Add profile section" menu we talked about earlier, there are lots of additional things you can include on your page. There is an option to add "Accomplishments" where you can list certifications, awards, if you speak other languages, completed coursework or projects you'd like to showcase. Maybe you've already taken some college courses in high school and got advance credit — that would be awesome to show here. This is another good place to add additional media like photos or videos as well. In the "Background" section, you can add volunteer experience. The shared organizations you volunteer with are an excellent way to connect with someone on LinkedIn. There's also a section where you can add your interests as well. It's been repeated many times over the years but still rings true today — people do business with people they know, like and trust. So anything you can add to your profile that might help to find commonality with someone else is only going to help your networking experience on the platform.

One other profile add-on I would highly recommend is to customize your LinkedIn URL. When someone searches for you on the web and your (completed) LinkedIn profile pops up, the link to the profile usually looks something like this:

https://www.linkedin.com/in/john-smith-21974414

It's usually some version of your name and a collection of seemingly random numbers. When you customize your URL, it becomes much easier to read and can better reflect your personal brand as well. Here is my LinkedIn link:

https://www.linkedin.com/in/techlifesteph

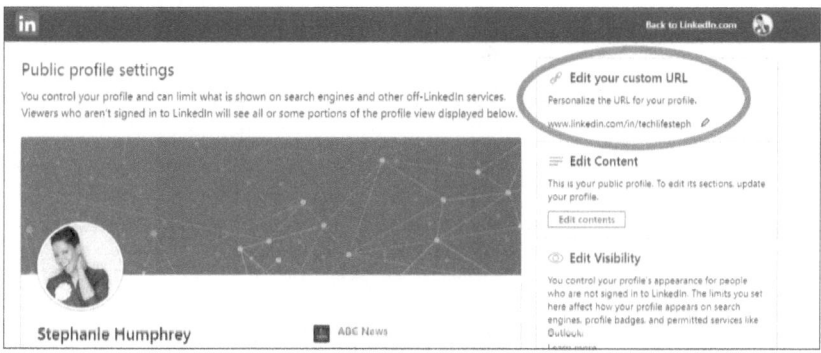

"TechLifeSteph" happens to be the handle I use across all my social media, and I wanted to be consistent on this platform as well. Also, if someone searched for "techlifesteph" online my LinkedIn profile (along with all my other social profiles) would be returned. By adding my name to a URL I've created two different ways to find me on the web, which increases the chance of being found by adding a little more optimization to my SEO.

ACTIVITY
Come up with a custom URL for your profile and update your account.

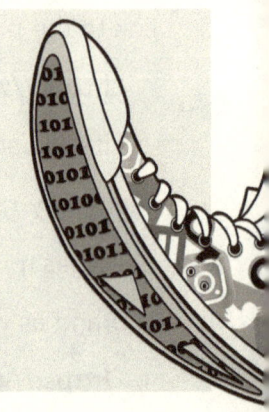

Content Is Still King

Now that you have your profile set up and are an official "All-Star," how do you use the platform to establish and grow your personal brand? The short answer is — engage! In addition to the people you are connected to, you should also be following others in your future industry as well. Following someone allows what they post to show up in your feed without actually being connected to them. The easiest way to get started engaging on LinkedIn are comments. You can and should "Like" and comment on different content that comes across your feed. Make sure the comments are relevant though and reflect the fact that you read the article or whatever was posted and considered it thoughtfully. Commenting on others' posts regularly lets people know who you are and can help when it's time to send a message or a formal invitation to connect to someone.

SECTION THREE

The next logical step up from commenting on others' posts is sharing your own content. An easy way to start is with content curation. Content curation means that you repost articles, blog posts, photos and videos from other people that relate to your future industry or speak to your personal brand. Include captions that will spark conversation and interaction with your connections. Even if the article has points in it that you disagree with you can still share it and talk about why you think differently — in a respectful way of course. Ask people how they feel about what you posted. And respond to comments when you get them — it can get overwhelming if you have a lot of connections, but maintaining that engagement is critical to the development of your personal brand. Try to set aside some time every week just for responding to comments or whenever you find yourself killing time scrolling on your phone, use it to reply back to someone that took the time to write something. Relationships get built using these tiny building blocks, so take advantage of an easy way to engage.

Once you've gotten comfortable with the conversations you participate in from the content you share, you might want to start creating your own original content. LinkedIn has a native publishing tool that allows you to publish articles directly to the platform. On your homepage, you'll see the option at the top of the feed in the box that prompts you to "Start a post" — see the photo below:

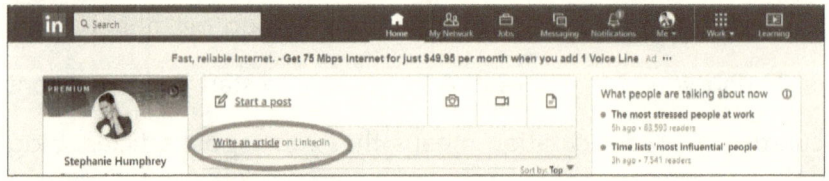

Once you click on "Write an article," you'll be directed to the LinkedIn Publishing page. It's a pretty easy interface to use and you can get started right away with your own original content. You can add hashtags to make your article searchable, but make sure your privacy settings are set to "Public" so that people can share your piece. The publishing tool is fairly no-frills for the most part, but it's clean and it gets the job done. If you already have a website or blog that you publish to regularly, it might be more useful to copy/paste articles from there into LinkedIn's publisher rather than just link to your site in an update. Articles posted natively to the site become a part of your LinkedIn profile and are more likely to be read and shared than links to other sites. You'll also be ensuring that your specific audience is being targeted because you're already connected to them. LinkedIn also offers the option of uploading slide decks with SlideShare. With this option, you can also view presentations from top companies or experts in your industry as well.

    I'd also strongly recommend considering posting video content to LinkedIn. The site's native video has been shown to get substantially more views that written posts or links to videos on other sites. So uploading a video to your YouTube channel and posting a link on LinkedIn is not as effective as uploading the video directly to the LinkedIn platform. itself. Native video is video that is either uploaded directly to LinkedIn or created on the site itself. The key to videos on LinkedIn or anywhere else is authenticity — you have to speak your truth, or it just won't work. Your perspective is what you're showcasing to establish yourself as a future thought leader and expert in your field. Two to three minutes of your take on some aspect of the industry you're interested in goes a long way toward building your personal brand. And again, don't be afraid to take a controversial stand on a particular subject if that's how you really feel but try not to be negative. Regardless of subject matter or position, you want your videos to be as conversational as possible. However, the YouTube videos you've been making where you prank your friends or the TikTok dance challenge videos you upload there are NOT appropriate for LinkedIn. I will say that there are some TikTok videos that showcase some very impressive editing skills. If video editing is something you see yourself doing more of in the future, it might be worthwhile to add some of those videos to the "Projects" section under "Accomplishments" in your profile. And some of the makeup/cosplay videos there could be a good way to show those skills as well. But always remember that LinkedIn is a professional social network and should be treated as such. If you're sharing content directly to your feed, make sure you have a caption that explains why you're posting it to give people context.

You also want to share some of yourself too. We're all walking that fine line on social media between personal and professional and it's way too easy to make a misstep and overshare. That's the whole point of this book — to get you to think before you post. However, the old saying is still true — people do business with people they like. So let people see your personality in your writing and in your video. If you're sharing content that you can personally relate to, add your own story to the mix as well. People don't want to just feel like they're being sold something, so it's important to remember that self-promotion is selling too — you wouldn't want to overdo hyping up your credentials any more than you'd want to be shoving a product down someone's throat.

Other Considerations

There are a few other LinkedIn tools I'd like to highlight that you might find useful. Be sure to join relevant groups on the platform. There are professional groups for various industries, alumni groups, groups for different interests, etc. Joining a group on LinkedIn is yet another way to find commonality with others on the platform and deepen connection. LinkedIn Learning is a treasure trove of video courses on everything from body language to leadership to learning to code. Some of the courses are free, but you may need to have a Premium account to access other content. But it could be worthwhile — even if you take advantage of the 30-day free trial to soak up as much knowledge as you can.

I would also suggest checking out **university.linkedin.com/ linkedin-for-students**. It's technically for college students, but any student can get a lot of useful information from the site. There are job postings for internships — most of which are looking for college age students, but if you think you have what it takes, I say go for it and make your case with a recruiter for why they should hire you. You might be surprised — a company could make an exception because of your skills and bring you on in a part-time capacity. At a minimum, you can start establishing connections with people who work in the industry you're trying to get into, so you'll already have a network built when you're ready to use it. You don't really have anything to lose and you never know when an opportunity is right around the corner! There are also videos on how to interview and get hired and lots of other resources, including building your personal brand, a checklist for making sure your LinkedIn profile is up to par and networking tips. This is a valuable resource for any high school or college student and I strongly suggest you check it out and refer to it often.

There are entire books that have been written on how to build a killer LinkedIn profile, maximize the platform for your personal brand, use it to generate sales leads and any other pursuit of success you can measure. The goal of this chapter was to give you a few things to consider as you start or continue your journey on LinkedIn. I hope I've been able to convince you of LinkedIn's value — it's a social network I truly believe can help any working professional, and it's my hope that you'll take advantage of all it has to offer.

ACTIVITY
If you feel comfortable doing it, write an article or upload a video to your profile.

How to Use Social Media & Your Personal Brand for Good

Now that you understand the idea of your personal brand online and you know what your social media profiles should look like, what are you going to use them for? There are a lot of different ways you can manage your brand online in a positive way. Students around the world have created charities, started movements and become advocates for all types of causes. And A LOT of people are able to use their personal brand online to make money too! You can say what you want about the idea of someone being an "influencer" — but it seems to be a legitimate career choice that people are making these days — and doesn't seem to be dying down any time soon. And while some people have managed to have a successful personal brand by being known for something controversial or negative, those folks are few and far between. It is a lot harder to maintain a negative personal brand than a positive one. And who wants to be *that guy* anyway?

As you're thinking about your personal brand, you first have to ask yourself — "What is it that I want to be known for?" I have to admit I struggled with the idea of personal branding and it took me a while to embrace it — asking myself that question felt like I was asking myself why I wanted to be famous. It can feel self-serving and egotistical when you hadn't ever thought about yourself in that way before. And if you're introverted or simply prefer staying out of the spotlight, it can be even harder to reconcile the idea that you'd need to be engaged in what might feel like active self-promotion on the internet. However, building a personal brand isn't necessarily connected with being a celebrity or being famous at all. Celebrities and people in the public eye have well-known brands because of what they do, but that doesn't have to be your motivation to work on your brand. A big part of our lives is shared online, whether we're the ones to share it or not. And that connectedness does play a part in determining some of the outcomes in our personal and professional lives — positively or negatively. So when we talk about branding, we're talking about what you can do to make sure that those parts of your life that you share online accurately reflect who you are and what you care about. It's important to remember that future opportunities might depend on what you choose to share online, and other people can be affected — positively or negatively — by what you share as well.

Let's look at some examples of people using social media in a positive way:

It Gets Better Movement

In 2010, Dan Savage and his partner Terry Miller, coined a phrase that would be the start of a global movement — **it gets better.** Mr. Savage was inspired by a recent story at that time about Billy Lucas, who was 15 years old when he committed suicide because of regular bullying. And what started out as a social media campaign that eventually went viral became a cause that champions empowerment for LGBTQ+ youth around the world. They were able to turn a single YouTube channel into an international non-profit organization whose mission is to "uplift, empower and connect lesbian, gay, bisexual, transgender and queer youth around the globe." Since they've started, more than 70,000 people have shared their "It Gets Better" stories on the platform and 630,010 people — including celebrities such as President Barack Obama — have pledged to help the organization, support LGBTQ+ youth and take a stand against hate and

SECTION THREE

intolerance. To find out more information about this organization, you can check out their website at www.itgetsbetter.org, or follow them on social media @itgetsbetter.

ACTIVITY

Think about a cause you care about.

It can be a global problem like climate change or something happening locally near you, like trying to get new playground equipment in your neighborhood or starting an after-school art program. Create a social media strategy around your cause.

What is your cause?

_____
_____
_____
_____
_____
_____
_____

What social media platform would best showcase the cause?

_____
_____
_____
_____
_____
_____

SECTION THREE | ACTIVITY

What type of content will you post? Video, photos, etc.

_____
_____
_____

How often will you post?

_____
_____
_____

What kinds of stories will you tell to grow your following and get other people to care about it?

_____
_____
_____
_____
_____
_____
_____
_____
_____
_____
_____
_____
_____

Alec Brownstein & His Google Ad

Before we talk about this case study, I want to give you a little bit of background. If you've ever been on the internet, you probably already know how big a role ads play online. If you're using a website that you don't have to pay for, chances are that's because the site makes money by selling advertisements and showing them to you somewhere on the site. Google is no different — the company makes billions of dollars each year selling ads to companies.

When companies buy ads on Google, one of the ways they target people who visit the site is by tying their advertisement to a specific search term. For instance, if someone searches for "Jordans," an ad for Nike is the first thing they see. (*Side note: nike.com is also the first search result because of SEO, as we discussed in Section One.) Most searches for any type of product will return at least one ad before you see the actual search results. But if you notice, there are rarely any ads in the search results when you Google someone's name. Even celebrities don't typically have ads in their search results. Companies just don't think it's worth it to pay for an ad for a product that is unrelated to what you were searching for because you're not likely to buy whatever product they're trying to sell. So the same way you probably won't see ads for refrigerators if you're searching for "sneakers," you won't see any ads at all if you're searching for

"Selena Gomez." However, just because you don't see ads when you search for someone's name doesn't mean you couldn't see them. That's where Alec Brownstein comes in.

In his search for a marketing job, Alec identified five different companies he wanted to work for. He researched the names of the CEOs of those companies and bought Google ads that would appear at the top of the search results when someone Googled their names. Because ads don't typically appear when you search for a person, if you saw one when you Googled your name, it would definitely stand out. Here's the ad Alec bought to catch the attention of one of the CEOs:

Alec took a chance hoping that any of the five CEOs he purchased ads for would actually Google themselves and see his ad at the top of their search results. And it paid off! Of the five CEOs he created ads for, he was invited to interview with four of them.

He received two job offers and accepted a position with one of the companies in New York. The best part of the story? Buying the ads only cost him six bucks!

Alec was able to use his digital footprint in a creative way to attract the attention he wanted to get for his personal brand, and it resulted in a job. Some people might call his method extreme, but there are some easier ways to leverage your digital footprint in a job search. You should definitely be following a company you're interested in working for, but also follow/connect with executives, people who work in HR or people who work in the area you see yourself working in. Connecting on LinkedIn is a good start, but Twitter or Instagram might also be effective ways to have a more personal conversation.

Reddit Minecraft Suicide Intervention

Back in October 2014 a Reddit user posted in a Minecraft forum that he suffered from depression and planned to commit suicide. Almost one hundred other Redditors used a TeamSpeak room (a virtual room set up for internet voice conferences) to help convince him not to go through with it, and dozens of others posted comments in support. Because of their efforts, the young man decided to rethink his choice and instead get the help he needed from professionals.

It doesn't have to take a large group of people to make a difference in someone's life. No one knows the exact moment when that young person changed his mind. No one knows if it was the outpouring of support he received or one specific comment that made the difference. But how awesome would it have been if your comment was a part of the conversation that helped save someone's life?! You can use the power of the internet to support and uplift others just by liking a post. However, I'm sure there were still trolls in that same forum who didn't have anything positive to say. Whatever their motivation was — whether they thought he was joking so they didn't take him seriously, or they simply wanted to be mean — their comments could have had a deadly effect on the situation. Like we talked about in Section Two, you don't have to put yourself out there to support someone if you don't feel comfortable doing that, but you also never have to add anything negative to the conversation either. **You don't have to add to the noise.**

University of Delaware Social Media Ambassador Program

Building a personal brand online and becoming an influencer aren't necessarily the same thing, but what if you could combine the two and have an awesome college experience at the same time? The University of Delaware started a program in 2011 that continues to this day that will allow you to do just that. The social media ambassador program was created to get students to share the school's story from their unique perspective. As a part of the program, students get free school merch and swag, front row tickets to watch sporting or other events and VIP access to meet high-profile guests of the university, among other perks. The students are also getting professional social media management experience before they graduate so they'll have relevant skills to add to their resumes. It's an incredible opportunity to network with others, be recognized around campus and build a personal brand. But the university isn't just giving any one a chance to become an ambassador. They have an extensive application process that includes giving them access to see your personal social media accounts for a period of time before they make their decision. Think about your personal online profiles. Is there anything about them that would come into conflict with a university's brand and prevent you from taking advantage of an opportunity like this one? A lot of other schools have similar ambassador programs. And while this may not necessarily be your thing, it's still one more example of how your digital footprint can affect your personal brand and any potential future opportunities.

Making Money with Your Brand Online

There is no shortage of stories about people who have been able to leverage their personal brands to make money using the internet and social media. Whether it's Kylie Jenner — who makes more than $1 million per post or Ryan Kaji of Ryan's Toy Review — who was the top earner on YouTube last year with $26 million or someone who might be making a few hundred dollars a month vlogging — social media can be a lucrative avenue if you have the right content. You can do unboxing videos, makeup tutorials, cooking demonstrations or just about anything else — the internet is wide open for anyone who wants to post.

There's no one right way to create content either. You can use your smartphone to create TikTok videos or shoot an entire show in a production studio. And content doesn't have to mean video — you can create a podcast that becomes wildly popular too. Or you can open an online store and offer products for sale. The point is that the opportunities are endless when it comes to the internet. But all of that freedom comes with risks and responsibilities as well. Here are a few things to think about if you're considering a career online:

- ▸ Think about why you want to do it — if money is your only motivation, it's going to be hard to sustain the level of work required to be successful. That goes for anything in life, but especially online where you might need to come up with interesting things to post every day or spend long hours recording content to grow your following. Becoming an influencer and making money online is a huge commitment.
- ▸ Think about what type of content you'll post — if you become known for posting stunt/joke videos, it's going to be hard to keep leveling up to more engaging content with-

out potentially hurting yourself/others or seriously offending other people.

- Think about what type of response you can expect — you'll need a public profile to grow an audience big enough to monetize, and there will always be people with negative opinions. Even positive attention can become overwhelming if you become really popular. Consider disabling comments on whichever platforms you use to discourage trolls.
- Think about your personal brand — anything you do online or in real life will have an effect on your brand which could impact your ability to earn money.

It's not necessarily a bad thing to want to become a vlogger or an influencer and make money online. But you have to understand the work involved, the risks involved, and you want to make sure you're not so focused on this one thing that you forget about everything else. Family, friends, school and other activities are just as important in life as social media!

ACTIVITY

Come up with an idea to make money online using your personal brand.

If the idea is something you really want to do, get your parent's permission first — you can show them this activity as a starting point.

What is the idea?

_____
_____
_____
_____
_____
_____
_____

What platform(s) would you use to promote it?

_____
_____
_____
_____
_____
_____

What tools do you need to create content/make products?

_____
_____
_____
_____
_____

How often do you think you need to post?

_____
_____

What are the requirements to monetize content on the platform you're using?

_____
_____
_____
_____
_____
_____
_____
_____
_____
_____
_____

SECTION THREE

Think About Your "Why"

Congrats — you made it to the end of this book! I hope you know a little more now than you did before about your digital footprint. The fact that it includes all of your electronically connected activity is the one of the most important takeaways of this book. Your emails, text messages, Google searches and social media posts (and a lot more) are all things that become *searchable and recoverable* once they hit the web. Your digital footprint then goes on to inform your personal brand online. But don't forget — your personal brand is represented by more than just your online activity. How you behave in person, what your written communication looks like and how other people perceive you all factor in to how your personal brand is created.

We've spent a whole book helping you to make sure your digital footprint is pointing in the right direction and will lead you to a personal brand that you can take advantage of. But even as you're considering your brand online, I also want you to think about WHY you post. There is a specific motivation for everything you do in life and posting online is no exception. Even if you only did something because you were bored or even if you don't consciously know the reason you did something, that reason still exists. That's what I want you to think about when you post something online. Why am I posting this? What do I hope to gain from posting? Who might I hurt if I post this?

You have a lot of different reasons for posting. Maybe you're feeling bad about yourself today and the likes you get on your selfie will boost your mood. That's cool — we can all use a word of encouragement sometimes — but make sure you're not basing your entire self-esteem on what people on the internet think about you. Maybe you've read this book and want to build your personal brand online so you can get into a good school. That's a good place to start but remember that good grades and extracurricular activities are still just as important as your LinkedIn page. Maybe you want to become an influencer so you can make money online. That's not a bad goal either but make sure you're not doing offensive or dangerous things just for clicks. Maybe you want to get back at that person who embarrassed you in class, so you create a fake account to post mean things about them. This book can't stop you from doing that (although you really shouldn't), but I hope I've helped you understand that there are some very negative potential consequences that can result.

The key here is to do your best to think about what those motivations are before you post, so that you can make a good decision about what you choose to share. And if it starts to get overwhelming, it's OK to log off for a while too. Your personal brand is important, but your personal well-being is the most important thing for you to think about. Are the things you do online actually making you happy, while not hurting others? It's easy to get caught up in an image of who we present ourselves to be, especially on social media, that doesn't really relate to who we truly are. Your digital footprint should be leading people to your authentic self because that's the best personal brand you can have!

www.ingramcontent.com/pod-product-compliance
Lightning Source LLC
Chambersburg PA
CBHW021408290426
44108CB00010B/445